Carving
the
Full Moon Saloon

The Art of Caricatures

Presented by the
Caricature Carvers of America

FOX BOOKS
Fox Chapel Publishing Co Inc.

Box 7948
Lancaster, Pennsylvania
17604

© 1995 by Fox Chapel Publishing

Publisher: Alan Giagnocavo
Project Editor: Ayleen Stellhorn
Technical Editor: Bob Altland
CCA Project Editor: Bob Travis
CCA Publication Committee: Bob Travis
Desiree Hajny
Dave Dunham
Dave Stetson
Special thanks to photographer Bob Pollett for his artistry and creativity!

ISBN # 1-56523-056-6 (softcover)
ISBN # 1-56523-067-1 (hardcover)

To order your copy of this book,
please send check or money order
for cover price plus $2.50 to:
Fox Chapel Book Orders
Box 7948
Lancaster, PA 17604-7948

Try your favorite book supplier first!

This book is dedicated to those woodcarvers who, like the members of this organization, aspire to elevate caricature carving to a position of greater appreciation as an art form.

Table of Contents

An Introduction to This Book

This book is about the *art* of caricature carving. It emphasizes the *creativity* of caricature carving rather than the intricacies of *how to carve* a caricature. If learning the basic concepts of caricature carving is your primary goal, then we recommend that you scan the titles of the myriad of carving books on the market. There are many excellent books available that will take you through the process of caricature carving step-by-step.

By the time you get about halfway through the second chapter, you will discover that this is a book of 21 independent chapters, each written in the carver's own style and each emphasizing the aspects of creativity and carving most important to him or her. Some will devote more time to creative thinking and sketching than to other aspects of the project. Some will take you through a mental exercise in blocking out a complex carving and pointing out the difficulties that might be expected in a project of this sort. The point to be made here is that we didn't strive for uniformity. Our intent is to share with you how 21 different carvers create a carving. We suggest that you study the methods and style of each carver. Pick and choose the information that will be most useful to you. By the time you finish this book you will probably conclude, as is our hope, that there is no one correct method of caricature carving.

As you read the following chapters, take note of how the approaches to developing an original idea differ among carvers. In most cases, the carver will engage in considerable research before embarking on the project. They study people. Airports, bus stations, shopping malls or, in this case, saloons are great places to observe characters in action. Printed reference material such as western magazines, books of western cartoons, comic books and newspaper cartoons are also good sources of ideas. Then, at least among this group of carvers, there are those people who find that ideas just naturally pop into their heads.

Once the idea is born, the approach to realizing their ideas in wood will also vary among carvers. Some will do extensive drawing, creating the character in several poses before developing the final pattern. Others will spend considerable time working the idea out in clay. Still others will do small test carvings before tackling the final carving. Their choice of tools varies from knives to large chisels to power tools. Finishing methods will also vary. Some will paint with acrylics, some prefer oils, and one doesn't paint at all. Recipes for antiquing will also vary. Regardless of the approach used in developing the idea and completing the carving, the end result is the same—a unique carving.

We have included patterns for each of the carvings in the saloon, and we encourage you to try your hand at some of these characters. However, we also encourage you to begin to develop your own creative abilities. If you are the type of carver who needs a pattern to tackle a new carving, then begin with some of the patterns in this book. But, be creative. Study the pattern and make a few modifications to suit your needs. Move an arm or leg to a different position, turn the head or change the expression, sit the figure down or stand it up. Once you become proficient in altering patterns to meet your needs you will find that developing your own patterns will become easier. That is the secret of creativity. On the other hand, if you have reached the stage where you are creating your own original carvings, then use this book to stimulate your creativity to new heights.

Have fun and keep on carving,
The Caricature Carvers of America

1

The CCA: A Brief History

On the weekend of November 17–18, 1990, a group of woodcarvers from across the United States met in Fort Worth, Texas, to discuss the possibility of forming an organization to promote their common interest, caricature woodcarving. From this meeting came the Caricature Carvers of America (CCA). The founding group consisted of fifteen nationally recognized carvers representing a broad geographical distribution as well as diverse styles of caricature carving. The newly formed, unique organization made no claims to being "the best," although the members were readily recognized as being among the elite in the carving community. They were widely recognized not only as top award winners, but also as authors and instructors.

Since that first meeting in Fort Worth, one member resigned and eight new members have been elected, bringing the 1995 membership to 22. The combined membership has garnered several hundred first-place ribbons, including many best-of-show awards, in carving competitions across the nation; they have published nearly 40 books on wood carving; and they regularly teach wood carving seminars throughout the United States and Canada.

The purpose of the CCA is two-fold: 1) to promote and elevate the appreciation of caricature woodcarving within both the woodcarving community and the general public through the exhibition of quality caricature art and the development of a highly regarded teaching program, and 2) to provide a non-competitive environment that will encourage growth in skill, creativity and excellence among its members and the carving public.

To achieve these goals, the CCA has embarked on an ambitious series of traveling exhibits and seminars. Their premier exhibit was held at the

These caricatures, carved by CCA members, were on display during the 1990 organizational meeting.

2

National Museum of Woodcarving in Custer, South Dakota, during the summer of 1991. That exhibit, consisting of 40–50 original carvings, has returned to Custer each year since 1991. Because this display has been the CCA's "lead exhibit," members consistently strive to produce their best work for inclusion. Although the members do not compete for awards within the group, the feeling is that no one wants to be embarrassed by producing less than their best effort. As a result the quality of the exhibit has improved each year, and dividends are being returned on their goal of personal growth in skill, creativity and excellence.

The CCA membership is strongly committed to education in woodcarving. In addition to the seminar instruction that all members provide on a regular basis, the CCA initiated a group-taught seminar in 1992 that was presented in Fort Worth, Texas, and Sacramento, California. The seminar utilizes the talents of several CCA instructors, each teaching one- or two-day classes of ten students over a three- or four-day weekend. They anticipate that this seminar will soon be offered in other areas.

To enhance their own professional growth, CCA members take every opportunity to learn from each other. A "creativity day" is included with each annual meeting. This is a day set aside to work on special projects that utilize the unique skill or skills of one or more members, and to have fun. Their creativity day at the 1994 meeting in Fort Worth, Texas, was utilized to assemble this scene.

From left: Dave Rasmussen, Steve Prescott (back turned), Gary Batte, Gerald Sears (with hat), Dave Dunham, Dave Stetson, Jack Price.

3

From left, seated at table: Steve Prescott, Dave Dunham, Claude Bolton, Jack Price. From left, standing: Dave Rasmussen, Gerald Sears, Dave Stetson.

Origin of the Saloon Project

The concept of a saloon scene originated during a summer spit-and-whittle-style carving vacation in Custer, South Dakota, over July 4, 1993. While enjoying each other's company and the great outdoors, several CCA carvers started adding unflattering accessories to each others' carvings. It was then that the idea of a group-carving was born. Perhaps a scene in which each carver contributed a figure would be possible. Naturally, a lot of questions arose. What would be a theme with which all would feel comfortable? Could we muster up the nerve to ask other CCA members to carve a piece for a group project? What would they carve? As individuals, we all had the same question.

Could I carve something that would be worthy? So many thoughts were running through our minds that we decided to kick the idea around for the next few months. Then, when the idea of a saloon project was presented to the membership at the next annual CCA meeting, held in October 1993 in Wichita, Kansas, we were warmly surprised at its acceptance. Next to organize it — quick—before they had a chance to change their minds.

A template showing the scale and pertinent supporting items such as the bar, table, chair and bottles was included with a letter to kick things off. Then during the week between Christmas and New Year's Day 1993, there was a gathering of the minds of the committee (and we use that term loosely) in Phoenix, Arizona, at the workshop studio of Dave Stetson. Stacks of cardboard cartons, several sticks of hotmelt glue and three days of uninhibited ideas unleashed the prototype saloon. There it stood, the CCA Full Moon Saloon. Wow, it really looked neat, even if it was only cardboard! And it was inspiring.

The responsibility for constructing the saloon backdrop was delegated to Dave Stetson. The prototype occupied Dave's shop table for nearly six months, taunting him to make changes or inspiring new ideas. Finally, with materials cut out and a stairway to nowhere stacked in the corner of the shop, he was ready to put it all together. Doug

Raine came up from Tucson to help assemble the pieces. They carved all of the railing balusters and doweled and pegged each one. At times it seemed as though four hands weren't enough. But, after two full days of hand-to-hand combat with the railing and stairway, the saloon was ready to stain. The bar back and bar were added and the whole thing was hauled off to Fort Worth, Texas, to the next annual meeting in 1994, for the final assembly.

"Assembly" day was a day to remember! We started at 9 a.m. and by 4 p.m. the scene was complete. Each carver was asked to place his or her piece in the saloon where he or she thought it would fit best. Our goal was to locate the carvings within the scene to most advantageously display each carving and yet create a festive, frolicsome atmosphere for the scene as a whole. Amazingly, everything seemed to just fall into place. A small committee pegged each piece into place while the rest of the group carved glasses, bottles, signs, and whatever else might be found in a saloon.

The entire project is designed to pack into a single crate for shipping and can be set up in about fifteen minutes.

The Caricature Carvers of America

Gary Batte (20)
Stephenville,
Texas

Claude Bolton (13)
Fort Worth,
Texas

Dave Dunham (17)
Cleburne,
Texas

Harold Enlow (3)
Dogpatch,
Arkansas

Tex Haase (21)
Tucumcari,
New Mexico

Desiree Hajny (11)
Wichita,
Kansas

Marv Kaisersatt (15)
Faribault,
Minnesota

Randal Landen (6)
Derby,
Kansas

Pete LeClair (22)
Fitchburg,
Massachusetts

Keith Morrill (18)
Brookings,
South Dakota

Peter Ortel (16)
Monroe,
New York

Steven H. Prescott (5)
Fort Worth,
Texas

Jack Price (14)
Cleburne,
Texas

Doug Raine (8)
Tucson,
Arizona

Dave Rasmussen (19)
Cokato,
Minnesota

Harley Schmitgen (9)
Blue Earth,
Minnesota

Dave Stetson (10)
Phoenix,
Arizona

Bob Travis (12)
Davis,
California

Joe Wannamaker (2)
Godfrey,
Illinois

Rich Wetherbee (7)
Colorado Springs,
Colorado

Tom Wolfe (1)
West Jefferson,
North Carolina

*Harley Refsal (4)

Full Moon Saloon

7

Full Moon Saloon

by the Caricature Carvers of America

With only a general plan of the structure of the saloon and notes about the scale, twenty-one members of the Caricature Carvers of America filled the Full Moon Saloon with a host of western caricature art. Most of the members did not know what the others were carving until the CCA's general meeting on September 23, 1994, when the Full Moon Saloon was assembled. Above: The entire saloon scene measures 4' wide, 2' deep, and 2' high. Figures are carved on a scale of 1"=1'.

Top left: Bob Travis' The Lady Card Shark *and Gary Batte's* Cardplayer with a Bottle *are joined by another of Bob's carvings at the card table. Above: Pete LeClair's* Cowboy at the Bar *and* The Cowboy's Sidekick *enjoy a frothy mug of brew at the saloon bar. Left: Joe Wannamaker's* The Dancing Couple *cut a rug to the music played by Dave Dunham's* The Saloon Piano Player.

Caricature Carvers of America

During their 1994 annual meeting, the members of the CCA were asked to place their caricatures in the saloon as they saw fit. They then spent the rest of the day carving a variety of props, such as bottles, mugs of foaming beer, spittoons and paintings, for the saloon scene. Above: A look down on the contents of the Full Moon Saloon shows how the caricatures fill the saloon.

Full Moon Saloon

Above: Rich Wetherbee's The Sleazy Girl on the Piano belts out a song as Dave Dunham's The Piano Player tickles the ivory. Tex Haase's The Bartender looks on as Joe Wannamaker's The Dancing Couple keep time. Top right: The sign from the Full Moon Saloon. Right: Claude Bolton's The Assistant Bartender serves up refreshments to Pete LeClair's Cowboy at the Bar and Desiree Hajny's Flirtie Gertie. Despite the sign, Joe Wannamaker's dog is enjoying a delicious free lunch.

Card Player with a Bottle
by Gary Batte

Gary, a resident of Stephenville, Texas, and an Area Conservationist with the U. S. Department of Agriculture Soil Conservation Service, is a self-taught woodcarver. His carvings are created from original designs and noted for their humor and detail. They have been exhibited at a number of universities, galleries and museums. Gary has won numerous awards at major carving shows, and his carvings can be found in many private collections.

Gary is a woodcarving instructor and has written a book titled Carving Critters, Cowboys and Other Characters. He is a founding member of CCA and a member of The Texas Woodcarvers Guild and Affiliated Woodcarvers, LTD.

Carving a seated figure is challenging because it requires a different thought process and different design and carving techniques than those needed for a standing figure. Having the arms and hands in different positions and holding objects adds to the difficulty and challenge.

PRELIMINARY SKETCHES. I thought that a whiskey-drinking, card-playing cowboy would be an ideal subject for an old-west saloon. My experience in carving similar figures helped with the concept, and the part of Texas where I live is full of real-life cowboys (but no saloons) that are good for ideas.

I began by working up a few preliminary sketches. This cowboy has just looked at his hand and can't decide whether to hold 'em or fold 'em.

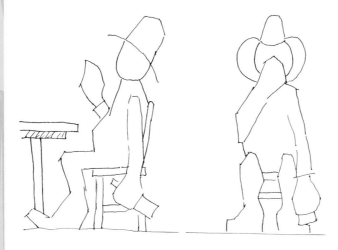

Once I finalized my idea, I traced a pattern from the sketches. I designed the cowboy and the chair together to achieve proper dimensions, but carved them separately.

ROUGHING OUT. I established the proper dimensions and planes through roughing out. A flexible ruler was helpful in drawing the center line, which I then used as a reference. Measurements were frequently taken from the pattern and transferred to the carving.

I roughed out the hat first. After marking the back of the crown and sides of the brim, I removed excess wood from each side of the crown above the brim; the front and back of the brim were then rounded.

It is important to establish the location and angle of the right arm during the rough-out stage. I marked the front and side views; then removed wood from the back, underneath and top of the arm, in that order. I carved the right hand separately and attached it during the finishing stage.

Before carving the hand that holds the bottle, I had to make sure the cowboy's bottom was no wider than the chair seat and check that the hand would clear the seat. Excess wood was removed from between the legs with a gouge and V-tool.

DETAIL CARVING. The seated figure must conform to the chair, and the feet must touch the floor. For this reason, I carved the chair first and then shaped the cowboy's back, bottom and chair

13

seat as needed.

Carving the left hand holding the bottle required the most study. After marking the side view, I squared off and flattened the bottom end of the bottle. A center line was then drawn through the bottle and hand. I carved the neck of the bottle next, leaving wood for the thumb and fingers. I rounded the rest of the bottle and then finished the hand to conform to the bottle. Carving the right hand and cards separately allowed for proper positioning when I assembled them with the arm. Enough space had to be left between the thumb and fingers for insertion of the cards.

The facial expression also required much thought. The partially open mouth suggests surprise or disbelief at the cards he is holding, while the eyes cast a glance around the table.

PAINTING. I wanted the carving to have a soft, just-off-the-ranch look. To achieve this, I used acrylics thinned with water. Raw umber was used to tone down the colors. I painted the trousers with a cobalt blue/raw umber mixture, using only a small amount of raw umber. To give a worn look to the knees of the trousers, I blended the blue while it was still wet. I used medium flesh acrylic to achieve the desired skin tone for the face and hands.

I mixed flesh with white for the fingernails. Vermilion was blended with flesh on the cheeks, nose, ears and knuckles. (Note: A mixture of red and orange may be substituted for vermilion). I painted the hat, belt and boots with burnt umber. The eyes are cobalt blue with raw umber pupils. To add realism, I applied a speck of white to each pupil with a sharp toothpick. The painted carving was sealed with a mixture of raw linseed oil and umber antiquing. After sealing and drying, I drew the designs on the cards with a pen.

Gary Batte's Card Player with a Bottle *(center) is joined by two more card sharks carved by Bob Travis. Gary carved the right hand and the cards separately.*

14

Card player with a Bottle by Gary Batte

15

Carrie Nation by Claude Bolton

Claude is a retired Texas educator from Fort Worth, Texas, who has been carving since 1974. He has written three books on caricature carving: Carving Cowboy Faces, Carving Cowboys, *and* Heads, Hats, and Hair. *He has conducted nearly 100 seminars in 20 states and has been an instructor at the War Eagle, Arkansas, summer seminar for several years.*

Claude organized the Fort Worth Woodcarvers in 1975 and is a founding member of CCA. He is a member of the North Texas Woodcarvers, the Texas Wildfowl Carvers and the California Carvers Guild.

My first thoughts for a caricature for a western saloon scene naturally turned to cowboys, gunfighters, dance hall girls, bartenders, musicians and card players. Knowing that the other 20 carvers were having the same ideas, I thought an opposite approach might be a unique possibility. Probably the person associated the most with the movement against saloons was the infamous Carrie Nation.

THE SALOON CARICATURE. Carrie Nation (1846-1911) became well-known for her efforts to stop the sale of alcoholic drinks. Although she was arrested often for disturbing the peace, she impressed many people with her sincerity and courage. She carried her temperance crusade from a level of education and organization to that of action and helped bring on national prohibition in 1919.

Her first marriage to a drunkard ended in the early death of her husband. Her second marriage was to David Nation, a lawyer and minister. They settled in Kansas in 1889 where an unenforced law prohibited the sale of liquor. Her first action was to pray outside saloons. Later she began to smash them, first with stones and then with hatchets. She was arrested often for disturbing the peace. The violent actions of the 6-foot-tall woman led to the closing of saloons in her home town of Medicine Lodge. She also opposed tobacco and immodesty in women's dress. She spoke eloquently and inspired others to imitate her. Her husband divorced her in 1901 for desertion.

DESIGNING THE CARICATURE. My first inclination was to design a very lively woman engaged in the activity of smashing the contents of a bar with her hatchet. However, as I drew preliminary sketches of such a scene, I became disillusioned with this possibility. One of the constraints on this project was its size. The overall scene is 2 feet wide by 2 feet tall by 4 feet long. If every carver designed an action-packed figure, the difficulties of packaging the scene for shipping would be beyond imagination. I decided that a relatively static piece would be safer.

CARVING THE CARICATURE. I have been told that purity in carving is starting with a block of wood and a pocket knife and carving what you see in that piece of wood. I am not a purist. My best tool is still my band saw. My drawing and sketching ability is also limited, but I try to get a good profile and front view. This way as much wood as possible can be removed with the band saw. My patterns are simple and lack any detail.

Both hands, the hatchet and the Bible were carved separately. They were not glued permanently in place. This allows the person who packages the scene for shipping to pack these pieces separately. A good tight fit can be accomplished by pegging them as illustrated in the pattern.

For several years I have tried to define woodcarving in four stages: good wood, sharp tools, an idea and practice, practice, practice.

Full Moon Saloon

In an effort to find a unique caricature for the Full Moon Saloon, Claude Bolton made this rendition of Carrie Nation, a woman who fought against the evils of Western saloons.

Good wood is always a premium. There are, of course, many kinds and qualities of carving wood. My choice is northern basswood, a clear white, fine-grained and firm wood, as opposed to soft heartwood or very hard southern wood.

Sharp tools are still a mystery to many carvers. Carvers frequently use only the tools that they can sharpen. Many excellent carvers do not use a V-gouge because they just can't sharpen one. Others use nothing but a straight blade knife. Others just use dull tools. The best way to sharpen tools—slow, but sure—is with a good firm stone and leather strop. Because I sharpen all the tools that I sell, I use power grinders and buffing wheels.

Ideas are often a problem for beginning carvers. The availability of rough-outs and a virtual limitless number of good patterns has posed a threat to originality. I have no opposition to either rough-outs or pattern books, but somewhere along the line a carver needs to do something that is original. Rough-outs, books and seminars are good for developing techniques. However, nothing is more gratifying than conceiving an idea and then seeing your hours of practice come to a satisfactory completion.

Which brings up the final point—practice. Golfer Lee Trevino said it best, "The more I practice, the luckier I get." Never throw scraps of good wood away until they are saw dust or chips. If you think I'm not a true disciple of this com-

mandment, then you just haven't seen my shop. If you see an expression that appeals to you, try it several times on wood that you would normally throw away from your band saw trimmings. Try it, you might like it.

FINISHING THE CARVING. More carvings have been ruined by paint than by dull tools. My reference is to the overuse of acrylic paints. If you use acrylics, as I do, the secret is water. Acrylics are strong. Acrylics are plastic. Acrylics can cover the very beauty of wood. When using acrylics, mix in enough water until the paint drips out of the brush and then add about that much more water. If this is not enough color for you, acrylics are "additive;" you can always add additional coats for more color. If you get too much paint, read the first sentence of this paragraph.

After my painting is dry, I apply a single coat of antiquing made from one part odorless turpentine and one part boiled linseed oil. I remove any excess with a dry brush. After allowing the carving to dry overnight, I apply a generous coat of water-based Varathane. I find the brush-on type is easier to control than the spray.

Finally, I sign and date my carving. Initials do not identify the carver. Vincent van Gogh did not sign his paintings VVG.

AFTERTHOUGHT. Early on in the process of selecting a project for the Full Moon Saloon, I carved a bartender. (See pages 20–21.) Then, after I came up with the idea of carving Carrie Nation, I decided not to include him in the scene. However, after setting up the saloon we decided that Tex Haase's bartender was over-worked, so we put my bartender in there to help pour drinks.

18

Carrie Nation by Claude Bolton

19

The Assistant Bartender by Claude Bolton

21

The Saloon Piano Player by Dave Dunham

Dave, a resident of Cleburne, Texas, is a Diplomate of the American Board of Orthodontics and maintains an active practice in Cleburne. His extensive studies in human anatomy have stimulated his interest in carving facial features and expressions.
His special interest is in caricaturization. He regularly conducts classes and seminars on caricature carving. Dave is a frequent blue-ribbon winner, and has won several awards at the International Woodcarvers Congress over the past three years.
　　Dave is a founding member and Corresponding Secretary of CCA. He also has held offices in the Affiliated Woodcarvers, Ltd. of Davenport, Iowa, the Texas Woodcarvers Guild.

An old western saloon wouldn't be complete without a piano player. Since I wanted to make a slight departure from my usual cowboy figures, I chose to do a piano player and his "Rinky-Tink" piano for this project. Rich Wetherbee agreed to collaborate in this endeavor by carving the dance hall girl sitting on the piano. (See pages 98-101.)

RESEARCH. I began by researching reference material for saloon scenes of the 1880's and 1890's Old West with special reference to musicians of that era, their clothing, styles and special features. In most of the old Western movies that I can recall, and in photographs and other references, the saloon piano players were usually dressed as Easterners, as though they had recently migrated West, either as adventurers or fugitives. I wanted the piano player in this scene to convey that image, thus, the non-Western dress, hair style and sense of grooming not expected in the typical cowboy or mountain man of that period.

DESIGN. I also wanted the character to display a vitality of movement, rather than appearing as a stick figure perched in front of a piano. To accomplish this, I designed him to portray the type of movement and actions that you might see a Jerry Lee Lewis or a Liberace make when playing the piano. First, I sketched a stick figure of the piano player and a piano to get a working idea and a preliminary plan for the piece. I then elaborated on my stick figure as to facial features, body position

and clothing. Finally, I wanted to unify this scene-within-a-scene. Since my research indicated that many bandstands/stages were placed on an elevated platform, I added a base. However, when we put the final scene together the base really didn't fit in the saloon, so it was omitted. The design progressed from a simple stick figure, to a three-dimensional artist's mannequin, and then to a final drawing of the entire scene.

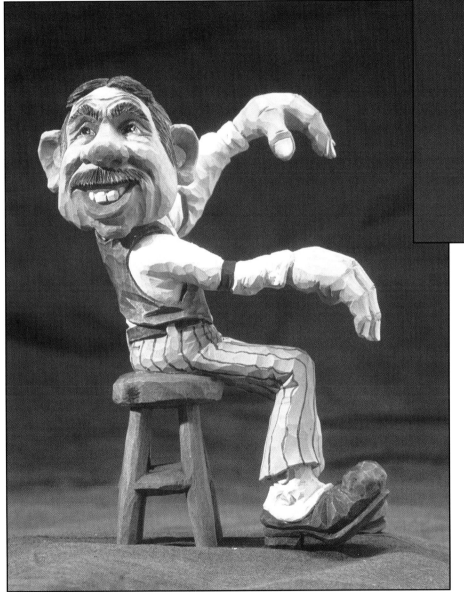

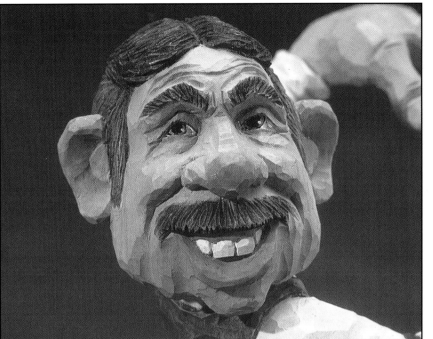

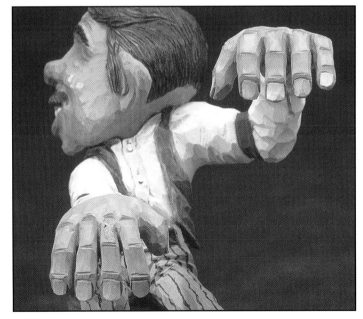

23

and beginning the actual carving of the piece. After bandsawing the figure, I felt that the cantilevered left arm, in cross grain, would need extra support, so I doweled this structure before the actual carving began.

The piano player and his bench are one piece, with the piano carved separately. I roughed out the musician and the piano to near-finished proportions to make sure that both pieces fit together correctly. The last step was the fun part—adding the finishing details of clothing and expression, painting, and consolidating the individual pieces into a unified structure.

POTENTIAL PROBLEMS AND SOLUTIONS. Obviously, design of a complicated figure such as this taxes one's three-dimensional visualization powers. A model of some sort would be a great help. You might want to review the information on clay models discussed in some of the other chapters.

I carved the seated figure and the stool as one piece to eliminate the problem of trying to fit the two pieces together. The carving is a little more complicated, but the results justify the extra effort.

The "pattern" is not a true band saw pattern. The complexity of the piano player's three-dimensional position precludes anything but some general rough shaping. This approach ensures that plenty of wood remains to allow for correct placement of all appendages. Your creative abilities will be tested in constructing this figure.

24

MODEL. A clay mock-up of the complete scene would have been helpful. In this case, however, I had enough working drawings to be able to mentally visualize the piece without a three-dimensional model.

CARVING. From this point it was a matter of sketching the pattern on the wood, bandsawing,

Dave Dunham's The Saloon Piano Player *was carved with his hands in mid-song to portray the vibrancy of a Western saloon piano player.*

The Saloon Piano Player by Dave Dunham

Flat On His Back by Harold Enlow

Harold, who now lives in Dogpatch, Arkansas, was born on Friday the 13th smack dab in the middle of the Ozark Mountains. Although he became interested in carving while quite young, he did not do any serious carving until he was stationed with the US Army, in Okinawa. Harold began carving professionally in the early 1960's. Humorous hill folks, which one expects to see in the Ozarks, are among Harold's favorite subjects to carve.

Harold has written nine wood carving books and teaches 30-35 woodcarving seminars each year. He is a founding member of CCA and a member of the National Wood Carver's Association, the Ozark Whittler's and Wood Carvers, and several other carving groups around the country.

THE IDEA. When the club decided to do a complete saloon scene, I started wondering what I would do. It didn't take me long to figure out I'd do a drunk cowboy, flat on his back. Since I had already done some characters in the prone position, I figured it wouldn't be too difficult. The scale is small, so one-inch thick wood worked well. This guy passed out in the middle of a conversation (probably with himself). You can tell by his left hand that he was making an important point just before he hit the floor.

It wasn't hard to come up with the idea for this cowboy. All I had to do was put myself in his place in the saloon and figure out what I would be doing. Since I've never been in a saloon (smile), I had to imagine very hard. That gave me a headache, of course.

I would have no control over the action of my right arm if my hand were wrapped around a cylindrical object, such as a mug handle or cold bottle, so I would naturally drink too much. This would put me flat on my back with my mouth wide open. Certainly I would be dreaming of my wife, Elaine, about the time I hit the floor. She would take on the persona of a saloon girl who would be pouring hot coffee into my mouth out of a steaming pot. This, being a kind and merciful gesture on her part, would tug at the heart strings of the most hardened among us.

As you can see, I didn't have time to do the girl, so out of the goodness of his heart, Tom Wolfe, in his great sorrow for my not getting her completed, decided to help me. He carved *Man's Best Friend* to take the place of the girl. (See pages 102–105.) Unfortunately, the dog is more handsome. More handsome than the cowboy, but you knew what I meant.

THE PATTERN. When doing a pattern, just turn on the movie screen inside your head and watch the pictures form of the subject you are imagining. You can move things around (they are now trying to make computers do this) until you have something you want. This isn't hard for most folks. What is hard is trying to make your hand do on paper what your brain just visualized. ##*@++%^&!

You have to try, so you might as well start. The first sketch is usually rough, so you try again. I have this neat light box on a desk I built, which Elaine won't let me keep in the house. It doesn't

Full Moon Saloon

look like much, but it is great for working on a pattern. You can trace the picture over as many times as you need to get it ready for use. Admittedly, this uses up quite a lot of paper, which means less wood for future generations to carve on. Drat! Always a downside to everything.

Seldom do I work in clay, but I do keep some around just in case I get into a bind. Since this project isn't very hard, the clay wasn't needed. A project has to get really contorted before my search for clay starts.

CARVING. The wood is only one-inch thick, so only the front view needs to be bandsawed. All the back parts of the figure can be rounded some, but most of the work is done on the front. The portion of the leg that shows is supposed to have "Texas" hair on it. This is accomplished by simply poking holes in the cowboy's leg with an awl before or after painting. I'm kidding about the Texas part.

PAINTING. I painted this carving, and that's the reason it doesn't look any better than it does. Elaine could have done much better, then Tom's dog wouldn't have looked so good. I didn't mean Tom's dog doesn't look good—you know that though. Acrylics were used right on the bare wood. Keep the paints thin, like stains, except for flesh, which is difficult to do this way because it contains white pigment. I make antiquing with raw umber oil colors and boiled linseed oil. Mix it to taste (I'm speaking metaphorically. Don't actually taste this stuff!), and add a touch of mineral spirits to help it dry quicker. Smear it on the carving liberally. Wipe it off with anything that is handy. I prefer cotton rags or paper towels. (Don't let your wife throw away that worn-out underwear unless they are silk.) Remember to dispose of oily rags in a sealed metal container or underwater as they may ignite spontaneously. This can cause a heck of a fire.

An Afterword from H. Elaine Enlow. Just this evening before writing out the above information, Harold fell while trying to balance atop a little bar on the school playground and landed pretty hard. We think it may have loosened his brain more than it already was. His thoughts, however, seemed lucid enough as he put them down on paper, so we left them as is.

Harold Enlow's cowboy, Flat On His Back, *toppled over onto the saloon floor in mid-sentence. Because his back rests against the floor, most of the detailing was done on the front and sides of the caricature.*

28

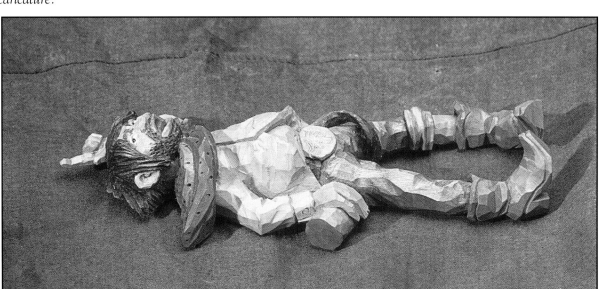

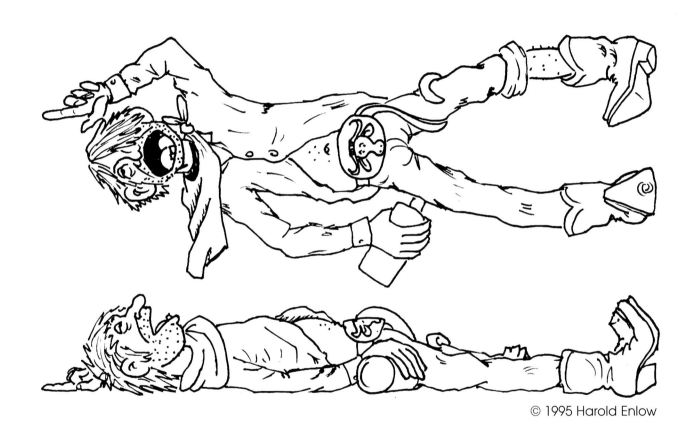

29

The Bartender by Tex Haase

Tex, a resident of Tucumcari, New Mexico, started carving at the age of eight. After high school, three years in the U. S. Marines, and a B. S. in mathematics, he began carving professionally. Tex expanded his knowledge with an M. A. in art in 1976. He has taught art and woodcarving at the vocational school, high school, and college levels in Tucumcari since 1976. Tex teaches wood carving seminars, judges carving shows, and is a frequent blue-ribbon and best-of-show winner throughout the Southwest.

Tex is a founding member of CCA and a member of the International Woodcarvers Congress and several other organizations.

I'll carve a bartender. It sounds easy enough and so it was... at first. Having been in a bar or two and having a bartender or two as friends, I figured this was going to be easy. I looked at some Old West picture books and mentally developed an idea.

PRELIMINARY SKETCHES. I sketched a couple of poses, but neither seemed appropriate for a figure standing behind a bar.

Because I like to work from models, I asked a friend to model for me. Two rolls of film and a couple of trips to a 24-hour developing service and I was ready to start. The pose I chose was a simple, straight-forward man about to pour a drink, eyeing a patron suspiciously.

THE PATTERN. The final pattern was developed from the above sketch. I usually draw a front view on my block of wood then cut it out on the bandsaw. I leave a lot of wood on my rough-outs in order to allow me to think out the posture of my carving and also to allow me to make any additions or changes that may come to mind.

FAVORITE TOOLS. Now the fun part. Being an amateur blacksmith, I enjoy making and using my own tools. My favorite tools are my knives, a parting tool, and a $1/2$-inch gouge. With these three tools, plus some small knives for detailing, I'm ready to start. As you can see, my bartender is probably the easiest of the carvings in the scene to carve. The only trouble one might have is carving

Full Moon Saloon

32

behind the hands, next to the body. Using a 7" x 1/4" drill bit made this easy going, and the rest just fell into place.

CARVING AND FINISHING. After sixteen hours of intense carving and a libation or two, the bartender was finished and painted with oil stains. Whew! Finished! Or so I thought.

Tex Haase developed the pattern for The Bartender *by asking a friend to pose for him. Models often help a caricature artist determine body posture and attitude.*

OOPS! Putting together the bar scene was going to be fun, and I was looking forward to seeing the ideas crafted by others. Immediately though, something was wrong. My carving was to the wrong scale. Leave it to me to make a carving three inches too tall. It wouldn't fit. Friday morning Steve Prescott handed me a block of basswood the correct size and a pencil and paper and told me to get to work. Peter Ortel handed me a knife and reminded me that we had our first showing the next evening at 6 p.m. So, while everyone else was enjoying making fluffy stuff to enhance the effect of the bar scene, I was re-carving the bartender. From 10 a.m. Friday until noon Saturday, when my new bartender was finished, this was one busy carver. Once again the group came through. Doug Raine loaned me his acrylic paints, and again the race was on. I don't enjoy painting, but I couldn't put it off and did manage to finish by the 6 p.m. deadline.

So, the second bartender presented to the group, a modified version of the original, is to the correct scale and is an exercise in doing something until I get it right. I'll pay closer attention to instructions next time and, as always, I'll enjoy carving and the friendships it brings.

33

Flirtie Gertie by Desiree Hajny

Desiree, a resident of Wichita, Kansas, is a wildlife artist specializing in the design of realistic carved mammals. She is also quite adept as a cartoonist and frequently carves caricature animals. She has exhibited nationally and internationally and has won over 70 first place awards, including 11 best of shows, since 1985.

Desiree is the American representative in the new international woodcarving magazine published in England. She is also a founding member of CCA and is a member of several other organizations throughout the United States.

THE DESIGN. Flirtie Gertie was a hoot to design. Attempting to make a horse look flirtatious and appear a bit seamy can be quite a challenge.

Many different thoughts entered my mind as I initiated the project. Does she need a saddle and a blanket?

SADDLE Study

Would she hang it up by the door to preserve the proper etiquette? Should she have a lot of make-up? Should I cross her legs...

CROSSED LEGS

or shave them? Perhaps put her head on her front hoof and tip her head...

TIPPED HEAD?

or turn the head? Should I make her skinny or fat? I tried several sketches and finally decided on a straight stare to make her look focused on her "prey."

Gertie was also designed to be redesigned. She can range in color or weight. (What, a diet?) Her head can be turned or tipped. Plus, her mane and tail can be short or long, curled or straight. So many options in one little cowpony.

CARVING GERTIE. Flirtie and the bar stool are carved in one piece. I transferred the profile of the pattern onto a block of basswood with the grain running vertically. By transferring only the profile, I have greater flexibility to modify the carving as I block it out. After bandsawing, I accomplished the preliminary roughing out with a Ryobi power grinder followed by additional shaping with a Foredom. By then, my power tools were a bit over-

Full Moon Saloon

Desiree Hajny carved Flirtie Gertie *and her bar stool from one piece of wood. She transfers only the profile pattern to the wood, allowing her greater flexibility when modifying the carving.*

heated, so I set them aside for a while and got out my large gouges. A little work with the large tools followed by detail carving with a knife and assorted palm chisels pretty much brought Gertie out of the wood. Final texturing was accomplished with a power rotary tool.

WOODBURNING THE PONY. To woodburn horse hair, make sure you do some homework. Attention to the flow is vital. Avoid making the hairs too straight and stiff. There are several books available on horses. Take time to study and research your subject. You will find it's time well spent.

PAINTING. If you are painting, use paints with which you feel comfortable. In painting, the artist must first understand a little about color and color vocabulary. For instance, when you read the following statement, what comes to mind?

"The value of a hue is made by adding one of the neutrals."

1. The neutrals are black, gray and white.
 a. White plus "color" is tint.
 b. Gray plus "color" is tone.
 c. Black plus "color" is shade.
2. Hue refers to the color itself.
3. Value is the lightness or darkness of the color.

To achieve a sad cowpony use cool colors. Cool colors are those that lie adjacent to each other on the color wheel and are somber or sad in feeling. Yellow-green, green, blue-green, blue, blue-violet and violet, also called receding colors, make things appear to shrink away.

If you wish to achieve a happy cowpony use warm colors. Warm colors also lie adjacent on the color wheel, but are exuberant or happy in feeling. Yellow, yellow-orange, red-orange, red and red-violet, also called advancing colors, make things seem to glow outward.

When mixing the colors for your cowpony, decide whether you want her (or him) to be sad or happy and mix accordingly. Mix either cool or warm colors into the main color of the pony. Use the tints (white) to highlight areas that the bar lights hit, and use shadows (black) for the shadowed areas. Have fun! The flirtier the better!

Gurls
ALL GET
Purdier
AT CLOSEN
TYME !

37

The Seated Cowboy by Marv Kaisersatt

Marv, a Faribault, Minnesota, resident, teaches junior high mathematics and has been carving since 1976. Marv's caricature specialty is unpainted figures carved from a single chunk of wood. His figures depict "ordinary folks doing ordinary things in exaggerated ways."

Marv is a founding member of CCA. He teaches several week-long seminars each year in Faribault. His awards are many and include honors from the International Woodcarvers Congress; the Upper Midwest Woodcarvers Expo in Blue Earth, Minnesota; and the Nordic Fest Woodcarving Exhibition in Decorah, Iowa.

Designing caricatures. That's why, after 20 years, I still get excited about a sharp knife slicing through a nice chunk of basswood. Taking an idea and seeing it through to its final form in wood gives an added sense of accomplishment. Designing and carving makes it twice as much fun.

GUIDELINES. I approach designing a caricature through the eyes of a woodcarver. Added to this are personal "ground rules." The main points I consider are: What tools do I have? Does the subject interest me? Does it still interest me? Does it *really* interest me?

THE SALOON CARICATURE. Off and on, over a two-month stretch, these were the steps I followed in designing the saloon figure.

1. Search for ideas. At this stage I plowed through folders titled "cowboys and frontier types," checked books for saloon scenes and scribbled notes from cowboy re-runs.

2. Evaluate possibilities. Often, on my two-mile hikes to school, cowboys and assorted cronies invaded my thoughts. They were all auditioning for a chance to enter the Full Moon Saloon.

3. Sketch. A series of stick figures helped me to nail down a choice.

The focus then turned to filling out the stick figure.

POINT TOE UP

6 GUN HOOKED ON CHAIR

4. Model in clay. Pushing clay around an armature allowed me to see a three-dimensional version of the design before the idea was committed to wood. At this point I became concerned about possible carving problems.

5. Revise the model. The hand holding the glass bothered me. I thought a little first-hand research would help. It did. Adjustments were made and I had a project that interested me, *really* interested me.

Full Moon Saloon

Full Moon Saloon

40

Marv Kaisersatt found carving The Seated Cowboy *quite a challenge. The cowboy, complete with his crossed legs, turned shoulders and tilted head, is carved out of one block of wood.*

CARVING. Carving the seated cowboy, with his crossed legs, turned shoulders and tilted head, challenged my skills. Carving it from a single block of wood added to the challenge.

BLOCKING OUT. Establishing planes for arms, legs, shoulders and the head was my first concern. Blocking out these major forms is the initial step in developing a credible base for carving details. Blocking involves: marking high points (H) on the band-sawed blank; carving from high points (H) toward key areas (K); and key areas becoming reference points for further wood removal.

Blocking out is shown in the illustration below. Removing wood exposes major forms of the design—in this case, the octagonal shape.

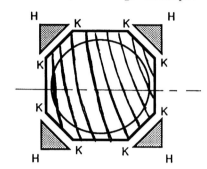

DETAILING. Carving details begins with a well-formed underlying structure. The foundation evolves as the blocked forms are gradually worked to their final shapes. Poorly formed structures at this stage will dominate a carving, even one with meticulously carved details.

FINISHING. I leave my carvings unpainted. The bare wood takes on a sheen over time that I find quite attractive.

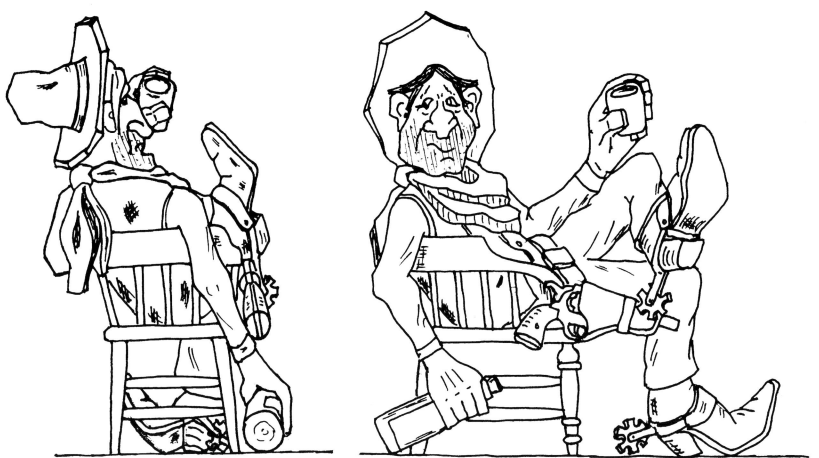

41

The Rail Rider by Randal Landen

Randy joined the Wichita, Kansas, Police Department in 1980. Currently he lives in Derby, Kansas, and is the Lieutenant in charge of undercover investigations and commander of a S.W.A.T. team. Randy began collecting wood carvings in 1977 while on his honeymoon at Silver Dollar City. Three years later the carving bug bit.

Randy is a member of National Wood Carvers Association and the Great Plains Wood Carvers. He currently serves on the Board of Directors for Affiliated Woodcarvers, Ltd. and the International Wood Carvers Congress.

As one of the newest members of CCA, I had the advantage of seeing the *Full Moon Saloon* assembled for the annual meeting in Fort Worth, Texas, prior to beginning my carving. Consequently, I had an opportunity to view the more or less completed project and to design my carving around the characters already in place.

THE IDEA. In my real job, I work unusual hours and often watch rodeo shows on cable during the wee hours of the morning. I guess somewhere in my mind, the visions of those bull riders and the thought of that long banister in the saloon ran together. As a result, I settled on the notion of a cowboy sliding down the banister like he was riding a wild bull.

DESIGN. When I first began carving, I swore I would never sketch an idea out or waste time working it up in clay first. I have since had to eat those words.

I am not a particularly talented individual with regard to drawing, as you can see by my original sketches. I started out with the idea on paper in stick form, and filled in the parts until I had a rough sketch of the cowboy.

From these sketches, I worked up the idea in a flesh-colored clay that remains soft until you bake it in an oven. Working the piece up in clay first allows most of the obstacles to be ironed out in advance. Unlike working in wood, clay allows for instant modifications in the piece, in as much detail as required. You then have the option of baking the clay for use as a model or for a rough-out pattern, or mashing the clay and re-using it on the next project. In this case, I made a fairly crude clay piece to scale and baked it for use as a rough pattern of the carving.

CARVING. I consider myself a "painfully slow carver." On this project, I was behind the eight ball time-wise, so I utilized the clay model as a pattern for a machined rough-out. Consequently, I didn't have to spend a great deal of time blocking out the piece.

I generally carve figures with the head on, meaning the head and body are one piece. I start

43

Randal Landen finds that exaggeration is the key to caricature carving. Enlarging the hands, feet and head helped him to give The Rail Rider *the look he wanted.*

at the top, carving the head and face first, and work down the project, using the proportions of the head as a guide for the rest of the piece. (Besides, if I have a particularly bad time with the face, I can always cut the head off and carve another one).

When roughing out the general shape of the carving, I try to use a U-gouge and a V-tool as much as possible. Unlike a knife, the cuts made by these tools allow for changes or adjustments without leaving deep cut marks in the wood. Once the general shape is roughed out, it's then just a matter of putting in the wrinkles and carving the details.

In caricature carvings, exaggerations are the key. Enlarge the head, hands, feet or anything which allows the carving to convey the message you have in mind. Authenticity is nice, but it is not essential. Toward the final stages of this project, I was forced to research the design on a pair of chaps before the cowboy could be finished. They may not be wholly accurate, but then, it's a caricature carving.

Some final advice on the carving process. Never sand a caricature carving. Sanding removes the sharp lines which give the piece character.

FINISHING THE CARVING. Being able to see the wood through the paint is important, so I paint using water-based acrylics thinned down to a wash. After the paint is dry, I utilize the dry brush technique to accent clothing and highlight some of the cuts. As the final step, the carving is painted with a mixture of boiled linseed oil and an oil-based brown paint (usually burnt sienna or burnt umber) to antique and seal the carving.

Be creative and have fun!

45

Rail Rider
CCA '94

R. Landen

Rail Rider
CCA '94

R. Landen

Cowboy at the Bar **by Pete LeClair**

Pete, a resident of Fitchburg, Massachusetts, has been carving since 1979. After tiring of doing ships in a bottle, he decided to try his hand at carving caricatures. He tracked down a couple of basic books on caricature carving, then after several years of self study, he finally got an opportunity to take a seminar with Harold Enlow.

Pete began showing his work in 1990. In 1994 Pete claimed Best of Show for his caricatures at the Susquehanna Decoy and Woodcarving Show in Pennsylvania, and then won the Texas Carving Guild's Grand Champion Whittling Contest open division, the first non-Texan to win the award. Pete was inducted into CCA in September, 1994.

GOAL. My primary goal is to have people smile or laugh at the carvings I create. This is why most of my carvings have oversized noses and ears. I don't work with clay, so I have to pay close attention to my pattern drawings. That's why I emphasize that the front view must exactly line up with the side profiles on my patterns.

TOOLS. I love my knife! I use a long blade (3 1/2") with a sharp tip for most of my carvings, swapping over to a smaller and thinner blade for eye and face details. I supplement my knives with a selection of palm tools, including a V-tool, small #9 and #11 gouges, and a 3/8 #3 sweep gouge.

DESIGN. For this project I decided to do a cowboy leaning against the bar and looking to his left. After thinking about it, I pictured a tall, lanky cowboy, with a weathered look. He's wearing work-worn jeans and shirt, smiling to beat the band and holding a well-deserved glass of beer in his hand. I began by drawing a series of stick figures in various positions. I then selected two of them to further refine into potential patterns.

Pattern A

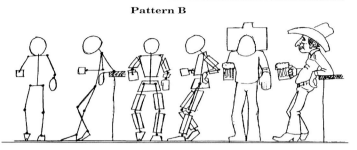

Pattern B

Because I don't work with clay, I reduced the patterns to 50 percent, cut them out on a bandsaw, and rough-carved the shapes into three-dimensional figures. It didn't take very long to do this because there were no details to worry about. All I focused on was trying to determine if the proportions and stance of the figure looked natural and fit in well with the overall scene. In this case, I selected pattern B for a couple of reasons: first, in this position the cowboy has a good view of all the action going on in the Full Moon Saloon; and second, a smart cowboy always keeps his back to the wall, especially in a room filled with these types of caricatures!

BANDSAWING THE COWBOY. From the preliminary drawing, I sketched the front and side profile patterns on a piece of cardboard. Next, I traced the outlines on a piece of basswood and cranked up the ol' band saw. With my blank in hand, I was ready to begin carving.

ROUGH CARVING. I usually begin my carvings at the top and

Full Moon Saloon

Pete LeClair usually carves his caricatures from the head down, taking several "passes" to complete one piece. A "resting period" between passes allows him to review his work and make adjustments.

work my way down. But before I even pick up my knife, I use a pencil to block out and shade in all the areas of extra waste (the waste stock to the right side of the left arm, for example). On my "first pass," I remove all of the shaded areas of extra wood mentioned above. This gives me the rough three-dimensional figure, but with 90-degree edges.

I again start at the top, and on my second pass I remove all of the "sharp" edges and cut in some of the general planes such as those for shoes, hands, and general body parts. I then start at the top again and refine the general figure a little more. I make as many as four or five passes down the body before I've got what I feel is a good roughed-in shape.

At this point, I stop carving and put the project in a place where I can wander by and look at it for a day or two. You'd be surprised at the number of minor changes that will occur to you when you do this. I also use this "resting" period to think about what I am going to do for details. Should he have a bandanna? Maybe a vest? If his right foot is on a foot bar, more of that boot will show....

DETAIL CARVING. Now the detail carving begins. This is by far the most fun, as it brings out the "real" caricature! The big problem with detail work is deciding when to stop. Again, I start at the top and work my way down, using my

old multiple-pass method. I like to get the face and its expression done right away, so I usually spend a little extra time on this area on my first detailing pass. I feel that once I get the eyes, nose and mouth carved, the piece starts to come to life; the rest of the body seems to just fall into place. Again, when I think I've got most of the detail carving done, I "rest" the piece for a day or two, using the time to mull over any areas that need further attention. Then, I make the final adjustments. These might include re-doing a few cuts that aren't as clean as I would like, or adding an extra wrinkle or shadow cut.

PAINTING AND FINISHING. Finally it is time to paint. I usually start with the eyes, using straight acrylics. The background white is first, then the pupils, making sure that they are looking in the desired direction. For the rest of the carving, I use artists oil paints thinned down with Watco Danish Oil (natural or clear). This technique gives me a very light-toned stain that allows some of the wood grain to show through. I start with a base coat of Watco and raw sienna over the whole carving. Then, I go back over with my final colors, starting with the flesh tones, and work my way down the carving. Again, I "rest" the carving while the paint dries, usually a day or two, putting it someplace where I can look it over a couple of times as I pass by. In some cases, I'll detect a small detail that needs attention, or a color that needs a second coat, some blending or a better edge. When I am satisfied that I have done the best I can, I sign the piece and call it done.

For this cowboy, I chose well-worn work clothes and faded colors. After all, this cowpoke is a working hand, not a Hollywood cowboy!

49

The Cowboy's Sidekick by Pete LeClair

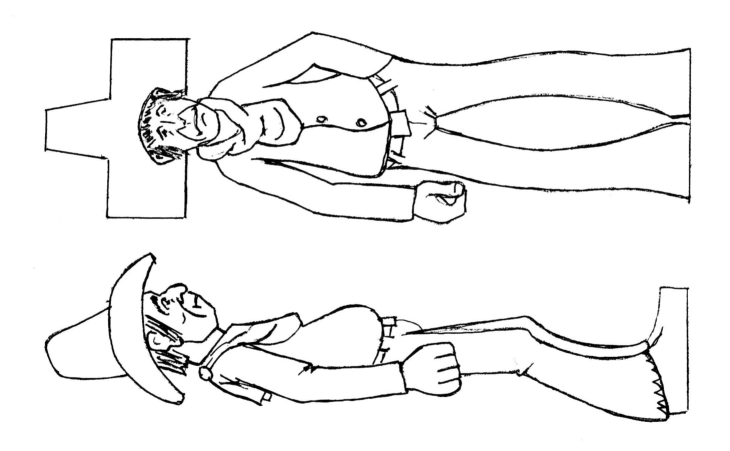

51

The Old Coot by Keith Morrill

Keith, a resident of Brookings, South Dakota, and a teacher in the Biology/Microbiology Department at South Dakota State University, has had a life-long interest in carving wood. Only after attending a variety of classes and workshops did carving become a "serious endeavor." While he has enjoyed carving a wide range of subjects in a variety of styles, caricature carving is Keith's first love.

Keith has taught carving classes in Brookings on a regular basis and has been invited to teach other seminars throughout the Midwest. Since 1986, he has been the summer carver-in-residence at the National Museum of Woodcarving in Custer, South Dakota. He was elected to membership in CCA in 1993.

52

WHERE DO I START. Where do carving ideas come from? There are a million ideas out there, the chore is to pull them in when you need them. Like many, when I first started carving, I carved projects I found in books. I still use them from time to time. Then I began modifying patterns to better suit my interests and goals. Also, like many carvers, I'm always searching through comic books, newspapers, magazines and other sources, filling file folders with patterns, pictures, drawings, descriptions and lots of cartoons. Get in the habit of filing ideas away and reviewing these files from time to time.

THE SALOON CHARACTER. In trying to decide what figure to carve for the saloon, I simply let the project roam around in my mind for a while, then I looked through my files and thought some more. For this particular project, not surprisingly, I had to abandon my first three ideas after learning someone else already was carving something similar. Then I recalled a cartoon of a drunk hanging on a light post—a hanging drunk. (See pages 56–57.) But there was no light post in the saloon. So why not hang him on the wall? Something seemed to be missing, however, and that's when I thought of including gun belts and guns.

The old cowboy in his nightshirt I call the "coot." I recall reading at one time in a humor book about the life stages a human male goes through. Most of us will eventually reach a stage

late in life that I refer to as "coothood." This is the stage to which all cowboys aspire. Tolerated, and at the same time secretly admired by other humans, an old coot is free to do as he pleases. The coot can wear what he pleases to the saloon, have whiskey any time he wants it and pinch the saloon girls at will without the dangers of physical retribution.

LET'S CARVE. Even with relatively simple figures such as these, I started with clay models built on a wire armature. Using a preliminary model allows for experimentation and change that would be difficult, if not impossible, if you simply started carving. While I have always done some sketching during the initial stages of creating a new figure, I find I am now more comfortable starting with a clay model. Once the body position is determined, then I turn to sketching in the details. This procedure seems to work well for me. Before finalizing the clay model of the hanging drunk, I made the wall board with pegs and pressed the figure into place so that I was confident the figure would actually hang against the wall as I intended.

When I am satisfied with the clay model, I lay it on a piece of paper and draw around it. I'll do this for both the front and side views. Now I have a pattern I can use to produce a band saw roughout. I allow for extra wood on the pattern in case I want to make some minor changes when I actually start carving.

Carving these figures is rather straight forward

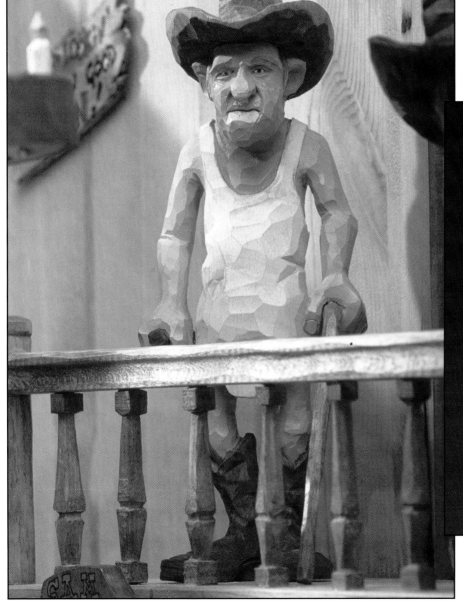

53

Full Moon Saloon

Keith Morrill found carving the face of The Old Coot *the biggest challenge about this piece. A sunken, droopy mouth and half-opened eyes gave Keith's caricature just the right degree of "coothood."*

because both the coot and the drunk are in a relatively upright position. What is the biggest challenge, and at the same time the most fun, is carving the face. The coot has left his teeth at home and therefore has a sunken mouth. I have tried to represent drunkenness by a droopy mouth and half-opened eyes that don't appear to be focusing on anything. If carving faces is difficult for you, and it is for many carvers, try a mouth or two and a couple of eyes on a practice stick.

While these figures are not action figures like some others in the saloon, they still require special attention to detail in terms of posture, the sagging limbs and how the clothing hangs on the figure.

I carved the gun belt by looking at pictures and by obtaining a real gun belt with gun and holster and hanging it on a hook. Nothing beats an actual model if available. Good luck with your carving. The main thing is to have fun.

©1995 Keith Morrill

55

The Hanging Drunk by Keith Morrill

The Hanging Drunk by Keith Morrill

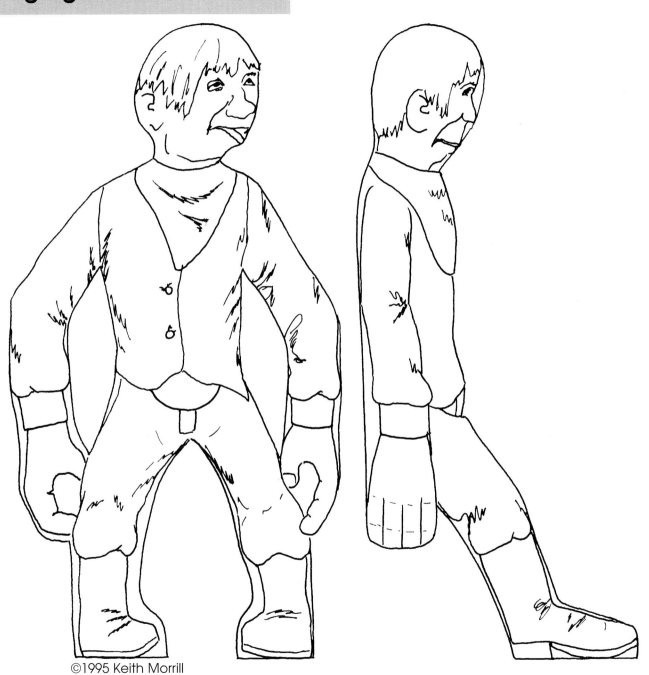

57

The Reverend and Mrs. Farkus by Peter Ortel

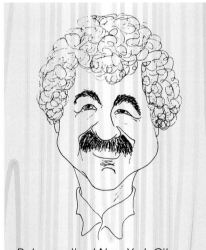

Pete, a retired New York City firefighter living in Monroe, New York, has always had an appreciation for all art forms, but holds a special affection for cartooning and woodcarving. Working in New York City, Pete could always find humor on the streets and in the firehouse and, when not fighting fires, he could be found sketching cartoons of the various situations he saw. Through reading books on caricature carving, he soon learned he could combine his fondness for cartooning with his love for wood. He took his first formal lesson in 1989 and was completely hooked. His imagination and humor are reflected in the scenarios he creates.

GO WEST YOUNG MAN! When CCA decided to do a group carving scene I was excited. When they said it would be a Western saloon scene, I smiled and thought, "Well OK, I've seen a lot of John Wayne movies with saloons in them." But did I really see them? Does a cowboy wear his pants inside his boots or outside? Is the knot of his bandanna in the front or in the back? Are his boots... Gee why couldn't they choose a crowded city street scene or maybe a subway scene? Hey, ever been to the Bronx Zoo? OK, OK. So that's how I found the Right Reverend Leonard Farkus.

Reverend Leonard Farkus is not really a preacher in a church of any denomination with which I'm familiar. The fact is, he was once a used mule salesman back East but was run out of town as a phony, a fake and a fraud. He sold so many

"lemons" that the Department of Agriculture wanted him arrested for giving citrus a bad name. Leonard earned the nickname Lenny the Liar and is also known as Farkus the Fabricator.

He was considering a career change when he happened upon a load of Bibles that had somehow fallen off the back of a Wells Fargo wagon. Being a rather resourceful fellow, he saw this was not only a chance to earn a few bucks, but also an opportunity to change his rather seedy image. He and Mrs. Farkus (the former Bubbles La Fleur) decided to once again put his sales talents to use by selling Bibles door to door. Somehow I think they're going to discover that they came to the wrong door this time.

So, next came many, many sketches on paper. Once a sound and interesting caricature becomes intriguing to me, I begin to use overlays of tracing or vellum paper. This allows me to keep the parts I like and change what I don't care for or improve on the figure over all.

This method does get confusing, so numbering the copies helps when there are many sheets. Next would be the job of creating a profile of the drawing, or front view if the profile is drawn first. The overlay system helps here also. With the paper over the drawing, I can mark off the main heights of the caricature, in a

59

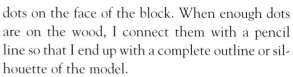

sort of point system, head-shoulders-hands-legs and any part that stands out from the figure.

When this is done, I'm usually excited and want to jump right into my wood block. But from experience and tips from other carvers, I've learned that making a clay model is a big advantage toward a nice finished product. I still have to fight the urge to start carving, though.

My clay model can be as detailed as I care to make it or as simple as I like, but each step allows me to make changes and corrections. Even while carving the block there are changes and adjustments made. "It ain't over till it's over."

When I'm satisfied that my clay model is the same as my final drawing, I transfer it on to the block of wood by either re-drawing it with carbon paper or using a point system.

THE POINT SYSTEM. With the clay model and the block of wood at the same base height, I begin by taking key measurements, such as heights of heads, shoulders, joints and hands. Next, I transfer the measurements to a block of wood by making

dots on the face of the block. When enough dots are on the wood, I connect them with a pencil line so that I end up with a complete outline or silhouette of the model.

Use as many dots (or reference points) as needed. This procedure should be repeated from

the profile of the model to your block. Make sure that you have enough of an outline drawing to ensure easy bandsawing.

Bandsawing needs to be done very carefully. Then the carving begins! I refer to both my drawing and clay model along the way. With a little luck, I end up with a piece that pleases me and looks similar to my original idea. If not, I just start over again. I've done that, too.

60

The Reverend and Mrs. Farkus by Peter Ortel

61

The Lamplighter by Steven H. Prescott

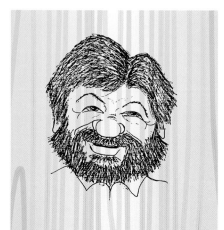

Steve, a resident of Fort Worth, Texas, is a junior high life science teacher with over 20 years of experience as a professional educator. He began carving in 1982 when his doctor advised him "to find something to do with your hands other than feeding yourself." Steve began teaching carving in 1987. He has won numerous awards in carving competitions, the most notable being the Texas Whittling Championship in 1990 and 1993, and has written two books, Cowtown Carving and Carving Blockheads.

Steve is a founding member of the CCA and served as its first president. He also serves as Regional Advisor for the Texas Woodcarvers Guild.

62

DESIGNING THE LAMPLIGHTER. I had several good ideas for the saloon scene, but it seems everyone else got there first or had a similar but better idea. I told Dave Stetson that I would carve "cleanup," meaning I would carve whatever was needed to fill out the scene. I wish I could say that this carving was a product of genius forethought and planning, but it is actually a result of Dave and me developing the idea in a process more accurately described as "inspiration by desperation."

This character began as a saloon girl on a swing, evolved into a drunk swinging from a chandelier, then turned into a lamplighter crawling on a rafter, and eventually to a figure clinging precariously to the beam as he attempted to put a candle on a wagon-wheel chandelier. Sometimes the best ideas develop by "brainstorming" with other carvers. A multitude of good ideas can be generated (possibly degenerated) by playing off each other. "Two heads are better than one." Of course, some might suggest that it took two of us to develop enough brain power to make one idea.

DEVELOPING THE PATTERN. Drawing a pattern for straight-up-and-down, head-straight, hands-in-the-pockets cowboys does not necessitate much planning. As you grow as a caricature carver, the more planning and idea development you do will certainly show up as a more interesting finished carving.

I had trouble visualizing the pattern for this figure because he is in the prone position with arms and legs extended or wrapped around the rafter. I used a combination of two methods to develop a pattern for this figure. I don't always use both methods on every carving, but I do find them to be beneficial when developing a figure that is intertwined with other figures or objects, in this case the rafter.

1. I often use small cardboard models that are joined together with brass brads or rivets at the

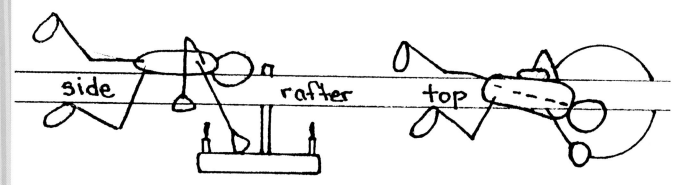

side   rafter   top

Full Moon Saloon

joints to permit movement to different positions. I have the models in 6-, 8-, 10-, and 12-inch sizes. This allows me to keep adjusting by trial and error until I get the figure in the right position to sketch a rough pattern.

2. I also use copper or aluminum wire to form a stick figure. Pipe cleaners also work well.

By combining methods 1 and 2, I developed a stick figure to show the basic design.

Clay can be used to "flesh out" the figure. The use of a clay three-dimensional model is very helpful in working out the "bugs" in a pattern. It does not need to be detailed, just the basic form is all that is necessary.

A three-dimensional figure molded from clay helped Steven H. Prescott to finalize the form of his caricature The Lamplighter.

BLOCKING OUT. Many of my students bring a blank to class that has detail drawn right on the bandsawed surfaces. By beginning this way, they will always have two reoccurring problems: one, they are afraid to take off the drawn on details and carve only on the surface; and two, they never remove enough wood to achieve a flowing structural form so their carvings will always look blocky, stiff and square. Remember, form is more important than detail. It won't matter how incredibly well-detailed the figure is if the basic foundation is flawed. I block out or round the figure to bring it to its basic shape before beginning any detail. I keep checking the figure for fit to the rafter or a small block of the same dimensions. I use a knife for most of the blocking in and a small amount of gouge or chisel work for hard to reach areas.

DETAIL. After refining the blocked-in figure, most of the fine detail is completed with small V-tools and a knife. Don't forget wrinkles at all the joints. Remember, there is a difference in carving clean and carving smooth. Those cleanly carved facets are like the facets on a diamond. They catch and reflect light and enhance the appearance of a carving. A "smooth" caricature carving looks squeaky clean and is usually lacking in character or visual interest.

FINISH. I use thinned acrylic paints to paint my carvings. I also use the standard antiquing solution of boiled linseed oil and burnt umber artists oil paint that most caricature carvers use. Minwax also makes a good wax finish that leaves a very desirable warm feel to the finished woodcarving and is easy to use.

65

Sal and Igoo by Jack Price

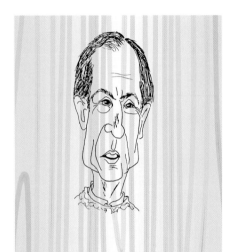

Jack, author of Carving Compact Characters *and* 50 Character Patterns for Woodcarvers, *is a retired Texas public school administrator living in Cleburne, Texas. He began carving in 1975 and has specialized in compact figures since 1978. Jack definitely doesn't believe that "bigger is better" as most of his carvings are only 2-3 inches in height. As he travels to display his carving talents, Jack is more than willing to share his carving knowledge with others.*

Jack is a founding member of CCA. He also belongs to several woodcarving groups and is past-president of the Texas Woodcarvers Guild.

66

RESEARCHING THE IDEA. The guidelines for carving a character for this project were simple. It had to be appropriate to a saloon scene, suitable for family viewing and six inches tall. Since most of my guys are only two inches tall, the six-inch requirement took me aback somewhat. I whined a bit, but then set out to find a character that was "fitten."

I spent several weeks looking through books that contained Western paintings, books about how people dressed at various times in history, picture books about trades and occupations, and comic books that had a Western theme. My interest jumped from one character to another until I found the guy I wanted to carve—the local undertaker.

A problem surfaced immediately with this selection. How could I carve this guy so the viewer would know he is a mortician? He wouldn't be carrying a tombstone around with him, and I couldn't put a sign on him. Yet he had to be in the bar with some tool or tools of his trade, and there had to be a reason for him being there at that time. I decided to give him an assistant to carry some of his trade goods, either tombstones or a coffin. Before going any further with this idea I prepared preliminary sketches for the two characters.

There still remained the problem of developing a reason for the two being in the saloon. After much thought the following scenario developed: This has not been a good year for the town's friendly undertaker, Sal Monilla. Folks have been rather healthy and death by gunshot has been rare. Sal needed to generate a little cash, so when the famous carver H. N. Low arrived in town for a short stay, Sal decided to take advantage of Mr. Low's talent and have him pre-carve some tombstones. But, first Sal had to convince the town's populace to buy their tombstones well in advance of their demise. Carrying a hastily-lettered sign and several tombstone samples, Sal and his assistant Igoo went to the Full Moon Saloon where Sal attempted to sell his layaway plan to the locals before all their money was spent on drink and other forms of debauchery.

THE CHARACTERS. By now I had a picture in my mind as to how each of the subjects would

SALE! SALE!
BUY YOUR
TOMBSTON
NOW AN
HAVE IT
CARVED B
THE FAMOUS
ARKANSAS
CARVER
H.N. LOW.
WHILE HE'S
IN TOWN.
THIS IS A
ONCE-IN-A-
LIFETIME

68

look. Sal would be dressed in a long-tailed suit with a vest and wearing a bow tie and a high-top hat. I envisioned Igoo as a slow-witted person in peasant garb. He would wear a collarless shirt, short pants that ended just below his knees, long stockings, and shoes with buckles. Both characters would have their arms bent at the elbow and extended forward; Sal to hold his sign, and Igoo to carry a load of tombstones.

PATTERNS AND TEST CARVINGS. With this picture in mind I made a three-inch sketch of each of the characters, transferred them to cardboard in order to make a pattern, transferred the patterns to a suitably sized piece of wood and rough-carved the characters.

The test carvings indicated that the designs required no major modifications, so I enlarged the sketches and traced the patterns onto a piece of two-inch thick wood. After cutting the waste away I was ready to start carving.

CARVING THE CHARACTERS. Both of these guys are relatively easy to carve. The main problems I encountered were carving the torso between the forearms of both characters and carving Sal's hands. In order to better visualize what Sal's hands would look like, I made clay models of each hand before carving them. This helped a great deal. In an attempt to make my guys a little less ordinary, I gave Sal curly, red hair and carved Igoo's hair over one eye. I also turned Igoo's head so he could look at his master.

FINISHING. Sal's hat, suit, tie and shoes are black. His vest is gray, and his shirt is white. His curly hair is burnt sienna. Igoo's shoes and pants are black. His shirt is hippo gray and his socks are lighter gray. The buckles on his shoes are silver, and his hair color is sepia. The skin tone for both characters is medium flesh. The cross tombstone is white, and the others are gray (one part white and two parts black).

To test his patterns for Sal and Igoo, Jack Price made a three-inch tall sketch of each figure then rough-carved them to that size. Once he was certain that he could rough-carve the figures with no problems, he enlarged the pattern to six inches tall and began to work on the actual carvings.

69

Sweet Betsy and Ike by Doug Raine

Doug began carving when not tending to chores on the family farm. At 16 he shipped out on a Great Lakes freighter and passed the time during off-duty hours carving small figures. After college graduation, he joined the U.S. Air Force and became a jet fighter pilot. He earned two combat decorations in Korea and again found himself passing time woodcarving. Doug later worked as an elementary and junior high school principal. He was active in Boy Scouting with his son, and camp-outs found him carving a caged ball and chain for the fascinated Scouts.

Doug served as president of the Southwest Woodcarvers and is a member of Arizona Woodcarvers, National Woodcarvers Association, and Affiliated Woodcarvers, Ltd.

THE IDEA COMES FIRST. I am often asked, "Where did you get the idea for this carving?" There are idea sources all around us. Photos of crazy plays can be found in the sports sections of newspapers. Check out editorial cartoons. I once got a great carving idea while listening to a CD of cowboy poetry.

My inspiration for this caricature came while browsing through an American folklore book. The picture of Sweet Betsy from Pike and her lover Ike gave me the idea. I would carve the figure of a sweet young gal rescuing her man from "demon rum" by hauling him out of the Full Moon Saloon by his ear.

GETTING STARTED. Although I have not personally experienced such an embarrassing and painful exit from a saloon, I thought there was potential for a lot of action with these two figures. I prefer to show some movement in the figures I

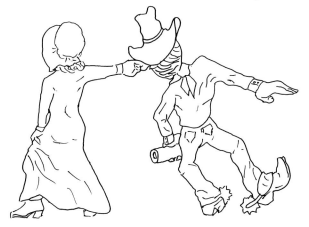

carve. Action adds a "fourth dimension" to a three-dimensional figure. It can be shown in a variety of ways—a turned head, the angle of the shoulders, a twist of the body or bent arms and legs. The figure design shown here is definitely action-packed.

MAKING A MODEL. Proceeding from a stick figure to a fully dressed figure was next.

I sketched in a few stress points and wrinkles in the clothing, then made a wire armature to conform to the stick figure drawing. Finally, I constructed a three-dimensional model with clay.

LET THE CHIPS FLY. I cannot stress enough that the one basic ingredient for a good carving is sharp tools. Every how-to-carve book I have read devotes several pages to tools and sharpening. Don't overlook it.

I decided to carve the figures separately. This

Full Moon Saloon

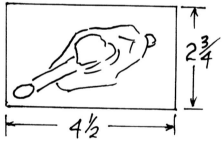

will allow for a slight swing of Sweet Betsy, a little to the right or left, to provide optimum fit in the final setting of the saloon scene. The outstretched arm and leg of the cowboy present fragile points and are strengthened by carving the hand open to grasp the bar rail, with the boot on the brass rail.

OTHER THINGS TO CONSIDER. For those who have trouble carving eyes, this guy is a natural. To show he is in pain, his eyes are squinting shut. His mouth can be opened in a clenched-teeth grimace, suggesting a lot of pain, or slightly opened to suck in air indicating less pain. Tight, thin lips on Sweet Betsy will show grim determination. Her thumb and forefinger are pinching, white-knuckled, a big chunk of earlobe.

Action figures cause stress points for clothing and present the carver with a challenge of showing wrinkles and draping of fabric. Having someone model the action of your figure will show you the wrinkles of the clothing and let you develop a more interesting carving.

Notice the drawing of Sweet Betsy is a $3/4$ view when compared to the full view of Ike. This view can be used as a pattern on a block of wood $2 3/4$ inches thick. When you do the rough-out carving, use your clay model as a guide and carve the figure at an angle across the cut-out.

Carving wrinkles in a caricature's clothing can give the impression of movement. Doug Raine had a friend model the actions of Sweet Betsy and Ike so that he could accurately carve the wrinkles in their clothing.

A BRIEF NOTE ON FINISHING. I used acrylic paint thinned with a lot of water (except for white). This allows the wood to show through. For the polka-dot effect, I used the tip of a toothpick dipped in paint. I used a fine point marking pen for the black lines on the scarf. I used Watco Satin Wax Natural for the finish. If an antiquing effect is desired, I mix a little Watco Dark with Watco Natural. I like the satin sheen this gives my carving and find it easier to dust and maintain.

72

The Janitor by Dave Rasmussen

Dave, a resident of Cokato, Minnesota, began carving in 1978 and has since studied the classical Acanthus style with noted Norwegian carvers and Dovre graduates. Using mostly basswood or butternut, his carvings range from traditional Norwegian kubbestols, to caricatures, reliefs and carousel horse restorations.

Dave received the 1990 Gold Medal for excellence in wood carving awarded by the Norwegian-American Museum in Decorah, Iowa, as well as many first place awards in competitions throughout the nation. He is a founding member of CCA and a member of the National Wood Carvers Association, California Carvers Guild, and Allied Artists of America, and an associate member of the National Sculpture Society.

DESIGN CONSIDERATIONS. When the project of carving a figure for an Old West saloon was first proposed, thoughts came to mind of all the old westerns. I could see Gabby Hayes, Buck Jones, Bob Steele and Tim McCoy riding the "B Western" ranges. What type of character did I like? Tall, short, fat, thin? What pose? Seated, standing, leaning against the bar? Letting my mind wander through the thousands of possibilities and selecting a few that intrigue me is half the fun of carving. The other half is seeing how close my completed carving will be to my original idea. The completed carving is usually completely original, different and one that has meaning to me.

BACKGROUND. We lived down the street from the pool hall in a small midwestern town. I spent many hours observing retired folks play cards at one of the tables in a corner, usually towered over by a few interested observers. As you entered the hall, on the right was a bar. A friendly, smiling "good day" was always the greeting from the owner, Spike Massey. Farther in the back were two pool tables with their bright lights illuminating the smokey darkness. Against the walls were a few chairs and a bench for the kibitzers to ply their trade. That was my pool hall, interesting, busy.

THOUGHTS. For my carving it seemed unwarranted to carve pool players. As for card players, would mine "fit" in with the others? I'd rather carve a whole table full, but we were asked to carve only one. A bartender? Possible. How about the guy that is always around the saloon who is helping out by doing odd jobs? I've scrubbed a few floors, emptied spittoons, dusted and cleaned up. Why not do the janitor? He could be working, but interested in what's going on. That's it! A character in jeans, with suspenders, wringing out his mop while leaning over to see what's going on in the card game. A rough stick figure sketch solidified the idea.

THE PURTNEER SPITOON mfg by "CAN'T MISS" INC.

Full Moon Saloon

Next, I filled in the detail on the stick figure to round out the idea.

See page 87 for another photo of this piece.

FROM IDEA TO CLAY. The scale for the saloon is one inch to one foot. I usually don't carve this size so I used a proportional ruler to get the proper measurements. Then I could exaggerate as needed. I modeled a clay form to give me a version to look at and to change as I wished. I also looked at the angles to see if there would be problems when carving. This figure could be carved as one piece, but I chose to separate the hands and mop head from the body. They would be joined to the arms later. This would provide easy access to the belly area and suspender attachments.

CARVING THE FIGURE. 1) I used the clay figure to draw my first pattern by holding it up to a piece of paper and drawing the front and side views. 2) I bandsawed the figure. 3) I checked the wooden blank against the clay model for head position and hand and leg angles. These are marked with a pencil. 4) Carving begins by blocking out the head, body, hands and legs, using the clay model as a reference. 5) Once the planes have been established, the detailing can begin.

PATTERN MAKING. 1) Once the figure is completed, I use this to draw a pattern to be used next time. If I need to make any modifications, notes can be made on the pattern for future reference. A side view, front view and sometimes a top view pattern are helpful. 2) I take a series of photographs to provide color reference and a carving guide.

CARVING THOUGHTS. 1) No amount of fussing and experience can overcome dull tools. I have been guilty of this when caught up in the fencing match of chisels and wood. Start with them sharp, keep them sharp and end up with them that way. With sharp tools, it's more fun to start again. 2) When carving, I work all around a piece, comparing it to the original idea and making changes as necessary. 3) Once the roughing out is complete, I use my pencil to draw in details to indicate where everything is, then proceed with carving. 4) If problems are encountered, I set the carving aside for a while, maybe even stop carving for a day or two. When I come back, the "problem" is usually solved. 5.) If bad wood or other problems are encountered, it is usually better to start over. I've spent hours trying to fix a piece and ended up with a mediocre result at best.

77

Hanging Harley
by Harley Schmitgen

Harley has been a woodcarver for nearly 25 years. A self-taught artist and enthusiastic instructor from Blue Earth, Minnesota, Harley has won top honors at many shows, including the International Woodcarvers Congress, the Silver Dollar City Showcase, the Upper Midwest Woodcarvers' Exhibition, and the Vesterheim in Decorah, Iowa. He is recognized as a master carver and is one of the founders and coordinators of the Upper Midwest Woodcarvers Exhibition.

Harley belongs to several carving organizations including the Central Minnesota Woodcarvers Association, California Carvers Guild, Minnesota Woodcarvers Association, the National Woodcarvers Association, and Affiliated Woodcarvers, Ltd.

THE STYLE. Welcome to the world of "thin" relief carving! The intent of this style is to create a carving that has an illusion of depth and roundness. In other words, it is a carving that appears to have been carved "in-the-round," but in reality, it is carved from a very thin piece of wood. The thickness of the wood used for this caricature is only one-half inch.

THE IDEA. In most of the bar scenes I have observed, there is some type of picture or painting hanging over the bar, usually a buxom woman. For our bar scene, I decided to incorporate a caricature of myself in long, red underwear to replace the female figure.

THE PATTERN. I began this carving with a basic sketch of a reclining male figure. On this drawing, I sketched a head with my facial features. I added holes to the long underwear and finished it with a pair of cowboy boots. Using carbon paper, I then transferred the drawing onto a piece of basswood 4" x 10" x $1/2$" thick. The outline of the figure was cut out with a band saw.

THE CARVING. I began by blocking out the carving and shaping the basic form. After the form was blocked out, details such as facial features were added. As I worked with the detailing, I would frequently stand back to evaluate the carving to make sure I was getting a three-dimensional look to it. This was accomplished through various undercuts with a knife. The three-dimensional look was also enhanced with a painting technique that uses many facets of shading. If the basic structure of the carving is incorrect, no amount of added detail, sanding or finishing could improve it. When all the steps are followed properly, the carving will "come alive" with a look that suggests that it has been carved "in-the-round."

PAINTING AND FINISHING. For painting my flat relief carving, I used a technique that is different from the typical style used by other caricature carvers. To begin, I "washed" the entire wood carving with a mixture of burnt sienna acrylic paint and water. This also served as the flesh color. While the wood was still wet, the other colors were blended in. The figure in the *Full Moon Saloon* was painted by blending a combination of red, burnt umber and white. At the outer edges of the legs and the body, a small amount of black was blended in to give a sense of depth. It is fairly easy to keep blending different colors while the carving remains wet. I then highlighted some of the areas with a well-blended white, which also gives depth and roundness to the carving.

When I was satisfied with the look of the body, I then painted the boots. These were shaded in the same way, using dark browns and blacks. A small amount of white was also used here to give a highlight to the center of the boots. The next step was the highlighting of the face and hands with watered-down burnt sienna. The final steps were

Full Moon Saloon

blending the brown and white for the hair, followed by painting the eyes and teeth.

After the paint dried, I dry-brushed the hair and beard with white paint to give it more depth and proportion. The following day, the carving was sealed with a matte finish spray.

The doors on the Full Moon Saloon balcony (green, blue, red and white) were painted with the same technique.

CARVER'S NOTE. To be a successful painter of woodcarvings takes practice, practice and more practice.

Hanging Harley *is a relief carving of the artist, Harley Schmitgen. His likeness hangs above the Full Moon Saloon's bar. The sign is only* $^1/2''$ *thick.*

Hanging Harley by Harley Schmitgen

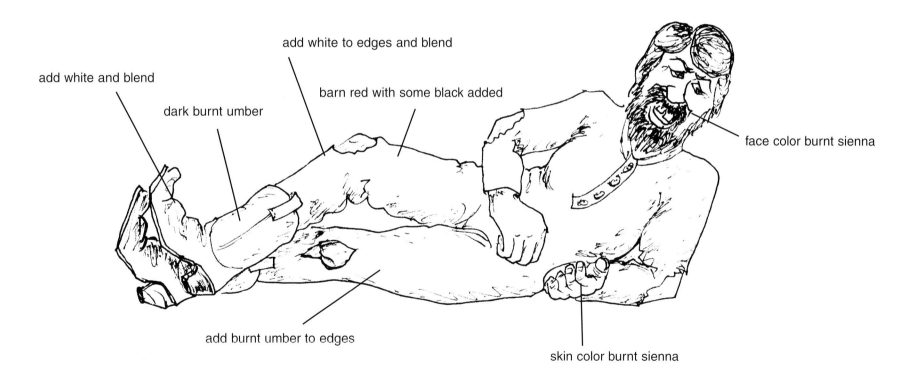

add white to edges and blend

add white and blend

dark burnt umber

barn red with some black added

face color burnt sienna

add burnt umber to edges

skin color burnt sienna

The Moose Hanger by Dave Stetson

Dave is a bookbinder living with his family in Phoenix, Arizona. He has a flair for capturing humorous situations with figures in realistic poses. The western influence in his creations is derived from an admiration for the endangered species known as the "American Cowboy." Dave has studied with other wood carvers, but is essentially self-taught. He now teaches his carving style to others in his Phoenix studio. He has won many accolades for his caricatures including two best of show awards.

Dave is a founding member of CCA and the organization's second president. He is also active in several woodcarving organizations throughout the southwest.

My journey into the world of woodcarving began when I happened upon a woodcarving club exhibit at a local mall. One look and I said to myself, "I think I'd like to give that a try."

I have been interested in western caricature from the beginning, but my early results were relatively crude. My cowboys looked more like corpses than animated figures. All I had to do was build a box and lay 'em in. In retrospect, I now understand that this was because the arms and legs were stiff and the head was usually straight forward. In short, the figures were static.

To counter this state of lifelessness, I moved to a new plateau, or to what I now call my Egyptian era. My cowboys had arms that were bent at the elbow, legs bent at the knee, and turned heads— just like the hieroglyphics on the wall of an ancient Egyptian tomb. Obviously, something was missing. How do I get the figures to look more lifelike? Real people just don't look like the paintings on the wall of an Egyptian tomb, at least not most of the people that I know.

The trick is to impart life into a carving. This is where the concept of animation comes in. It is not enough to simply bend an arm or a leg, or to turn the head to bring a figure to life. To be successful, one must take advantage of the entire range of motion that a human figure is capable of attaining. Following are a few tips to help you reach this goal.

HEAD. The head is generally the focal point of the carving. It can not only turn from side to side, but the neck affords it the ability to pivot up and down, even to twist. Good caricature will usually take full advantage of this range of motion.

BODY AND TORSO. The spine is quite flexible, allowing the body to bend and twist. To take full advantage of this characteristic, turn the hips and tilt shoulders.

HANDS. Hands can be the most expressive feature of the figure, but they can also be the most difficult part to carve. During my corpse and Egyptian stages, I usually stuck the hands in pockets so I wouldn't have to deal with them. On the other hand (pun), it is difficult get one's entire hand into a pocket.

SPECIAL TECHNIQUE. In my carving for this scene, I've tried to utilize these principles. Good execution will elevate one carving above the others. Just in case the others have done a better job than I, I've developed another, obvious, technique to help my carving rise above the rest. Can you figure it out?

SOME FINAL THOUGHTS. To create this carving, I started by asking my son to climb up on a step ladder and hold a garbage can over his head. This can only be accomplished by training your kids from early childhood to assume unnatural poses for various subjects; otherwise, they would

83

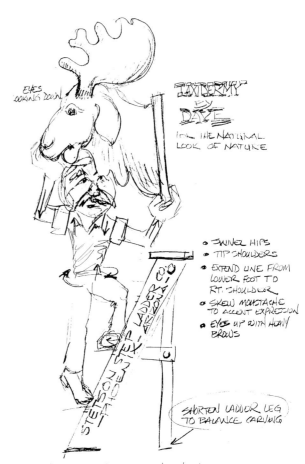

be reluctant to cooperate. The neighbor kids, if asked to pose, just look at me funny and mumble something as they walk away.

The actual carving started with building the stepladder. Then a wire stick figure, or armature, was bent to look like my kid on the ladder. After covering the armature with clay, I was able to mold a likeness of an older gentleman to use as my model for the carving. Many thanks go to Mary Duke Guldan and her book *A Woodcarvers Workbook* for showing me what a moose looks like. We all know a moose when

To make sure he was positioning the moose hanger's body correctly, Dave Stetson asked his son to climb up on a step ladder and hold a garbage can above his head.

we see one, but creating one can be accomplished only if we really understand what one looks like.

Caricature is exaggeration of reality. A distortion of reality is cartooning. Often caricature and cartooning overstep their bounds and move into a gray area between the two. For me, that "gray" area is where the real fun of caricature carving resides. If it works, go for it! If not, go back to the basics and study the real thing, for it is only through a true understanding of realism that one can effectively pull off a good caricature carving. Caricature is not a realistic carving gone bad. Rather, it is a realistic piece that has been improved upon.

The Moose Hanger by Dave Stetson

PATTERN FOR GUY
ON A MOOSE
HANGIN A STEPLADDER

The Lady Card Shark by Bob Travis

Carving this gal was easy, coming up with the idea was the hard part. I presume you have read most of the other chapters by now, so you know a little about how an idea evolves. I watch people, especially at places like airports and shopping malls. That approach didn't help much with this project though. I've been in a lot of airports and have yet to see a girl like this one. Books of western cartoons are another good source of ideas. With a little effort you can find examples of every conceivable character that could be even remotely associated with a saloon.

My first attempt was to carve a drunk. He's the one with the bottle, standing on the balcony. He turned out OK, but he just wasn't what I wanted for my primary contribution. Next I carved a card player with a hand over one eye, a disgusted look on his face and a lousy hand of cards. He also turned out OK, but he still was not what I wanted. I think I had too much time on my hands. We were short a card player though, so he's in there, too. Finally, I hit on the idea of doing a female card player, partly from seeing one in a cartoon, and partly because I have been carving and teaching the carving of cowgirls for several years. My original intent was to carve her holding a winning hand of cards, but to do so would block the view of her other "assets."

MODELS. If you have read the other chapters you know that some CCA carvers start out with a clay model. The reasons are obvious. If you work out your ideas in a forgiving medium first, you will probably throw away a lot less wood. Knowing that, I skipped the clay anyway and jumped directly into the wood. I was lucky. She turned out OK the first time.

PATTERNS. I began by sketching stick figures of each character. This gave me a fairly good idea of how the finished carving would look.

Once suitable stick figures were completed, I sketched the patterns for bandsawed cut-outs. Since the drunk appears in the scene, I have also included a pattern for him. The card player is similar to Gary Batte's. If you try him, use Gary's pattern (See page 15.), but move the right hand up to partially cover his face and place the cards in his left hand.

For complex figures with the arms and legs askew, I find it easier to work from a single dimension cut-out. Otherwise, I usually cut away some

Full Moon Saloon

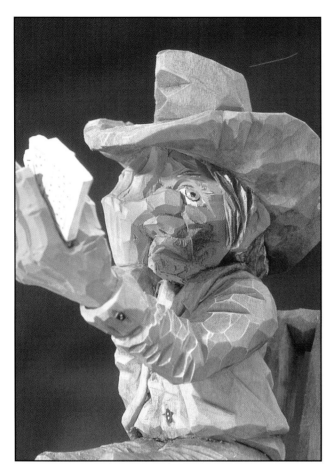

This caricature of a card player, also carved by Bob Travis, joins The Lady Card Shark *for a round of cards at the Full Moon Saloon.*

important part of the wood. For the drunk, a front view of the body was appropriate. When I carve a head separately, as in this case, I find it easier to work from a profile cut-out.

Because the girl's arms and legs come more or less straight forward, I really didn't need a front view pattern for her. The seated figure is a bit tricky to draw, but if you have a good understanding of human body proportions, it is not too difficult. The easiest way is to begin with a standing figure, then sit it down. This requires that you bend the legs at right angles at the hips and knees. Keep in mind that the crotch is in the center of the body and that the knees and elbows are in the middle of the legs and arms, respectively. In this carving, her breasts and buttocks rest on flat surfaces. Be sure that the pattern lines are perfectly straight in those places, and carefully cut straight lines when bandsawing the blank.

CARVING. I began by sketching in a few guidelines on each carving, then removing the wood with a selection of knives and small palm tools. For the drunk cowboy, the front view cut-out left ample wood to carve the arms and legs in any number of positions. Experiment with this a bit to find something you like. Because the head is carved separately you can discard the first few if you are unhappy with them. When you have one

you like, fit it to the body so that it is turned to one side.

The female face requires special attention in carving if you hope to eliminate the ugly cowboy look. Actually the approach to carving a female face is similar to that of carving the male face, but precaution must be taken to soften all lines. For example, when carving a cowboy, I begin the face by cutting in a deep brow line at eye level with a knife or V-gouge. For a girl, I make that cut with a deep U-gouge. Repeat the process under her nose, and it will have a cute, ski-jump look. The rest of the face is fairly simple. Just remember to keep it soft, no sharp angles. In teaching the female face, I tell my students that the difference between an ugly, homely or masculine face and a cute female face is usually less than a half of thimble of chips.

The rest of the carving of the girl is fairly straight forward. I purposely carved her head and feet larger than scale because that is part of my style. Her other features that are out of proportion were carved that way to give the cowboys something to talk about.

89

The Drunk **by Bob Travis**

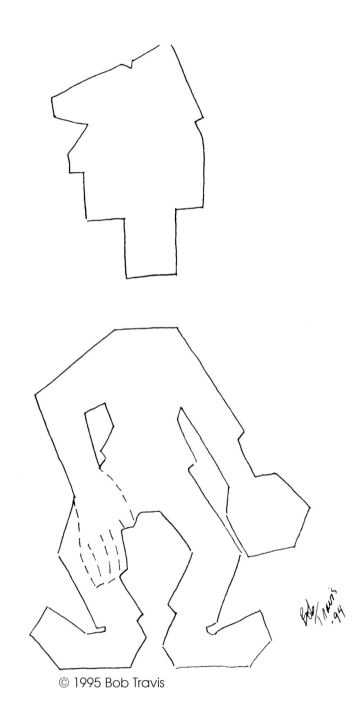

91

The Dancing Couple **by Joe Wannamaker**

Joe, a resident of Godfrey, Illinois, is an accomplished sculptor and does outstanding realistic carving, but he has a special flair for caricature carving. His carvings have won over 80 ribbons during the past seven years, including several first place awards at the International Wood Carvers Congress in Davenport, Iowa. Joe exhibits his work on a regular basis at major carving shows.

Joe is a member of the National Woodcarvers Association, Affiliated Woodcarvers, California Carvers Guild, and the Texas Woodcarvers Guild.

THE IDEA. When I found out that Dave Dunham had carved a piano player and a piano for the saloon scene (See pages 22–25.), I immediately envisioned a couple of 1880s dancers whooping it up on Saturday night.

I don't draw well, and I normally have a terrible time getting a single figure down on paper. Now, I was wanting to do "two" figures entwined in a very active dance. After my third drawing attempt, I was very discouraged. All I had was a crude outline of two people in the proper scale of 1 inch to 1 foot. Now what?

THE CLAY MODEL. There was no way for me to go but to make a clay model. As I made up the armature, it became clear that the dancers were so entwined with each other that they would have to be carved from one piece of wood. Hey, that's CCA fellow member Marv Kaisersatt's stuff and beyond my depth.

For my armature, I used aluminum wire from a clothesline with the plastic removed. Each figure

required three pieces of wire threaded through wooden blocks for the head, upper body and pelvic area. The holes drilled in the blocks were

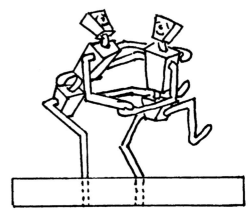

small enough to make the wire fit snugly to keep the armature from moving too freely. Each dancer has one foot on the floor, and the wire for that leg went straight into the armature base. After getting the figure bent around and into position, I put two-part epoxy on all the joints and where the legs went into the base. This made the wire and wood assembly rigid so that the pose wouldn't change as I pressed the clay onto it.

Anyhow, I fought the battle, and using modeling clay, I finally did finish a decent model. The clay I used can be hardened by baking it in the oven at 275 degrees for 15 minutes for each $1/4$ inch of thickness. This wasn't a flat cookie you could measure, so I made a guesstimate and cooked the sucker for $1^1/2$ hours. It worked, and I had a nice hard model.

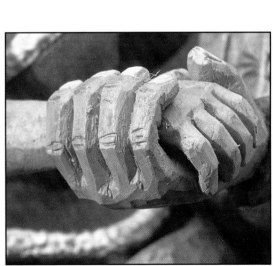

Full Moon Saloon

Joe Wannamaker's piece, The Dancing Couple, *is carved from one piece of wood—except for the plume on the woman's hat. The plume was inserted after the initial idea was roughed out.*

NEXT COMES THE CARVING. I also have a small duplicator, and I was able to use the hard model to rough-out the carving. It wasn't a beautiful, detailed rough-out, but it sure put the basic shapes where they needed to be.

I've always admired Kaisersatt's one-piece carvings, and now I found out how tough they are to do. When you get the basic carving done and are into the fine details, you have to turn the carving almost constantly. Belatedly, I realized that the lady didn't have a plume on her hat, so I added one and shot down the one-piece carving.

FINISHING THE CARVING. Sometimes carvings get pretty dirty by the time they are ready to paint. I usually scrub the carving using a clear detergent sparingly and a curved denture brush. After a quick rinse, I use a face towel to absorb excess moisture. The scrubbing gets the carving clean and will remove a lot of "fuzzies," too. I allow the carving to dry thoroughly over night, then give it a flowing coat of Bix pre-stain. This should dry several hours, again over night if time permits. The pre-stain seals the wood and lets the paint cover uniformly, even on the end grain.

When I use acrylic paints, I always thin them way down—way, way down. Remember, it is harder to get the paint too thin than it is to leave it too thick. Heavy painting almost always ruins an otherwise decent woodcarving. A second coat of thinned paint, where needed, is the way to go, rather than one heavy coat. I do use full-strength paint in some details such as the white of the eyes and teeth, and belt buckles.

If I had my druthers, someone else could do all the painting, but it doesn't work that way. If you are going to carve caricatures and enter competitions, you must learn to paint. So thin your paint and try to enjoy painting, and you'll surprise yourself.

AFTERTHOUGHT. Any half-way respectable saloon should offer a free lunch to its patrons. The proprietors of the Full Moon Saloon intended to do just that. Unfortunately, Fido got there first. So, as the old saying goes, "There ain't no free lunch."

95

No Free Lunch by Joe Wannamaker

Sleazy Girl on the Piano by Rich Wetherbee

Inspired first by his father, Rich, a resident of Colorado Springs, Colorado, has been carving since he was a child. He has had no formal training and works mainly in clay and wood. He presently operates a sculpture company in Colorado Springs, Colorado, called Wetherbee Studio, that reproduces and distributes his work nationwide. Rich teaches seminars in woodcarving and sculpts commercially for several art reproduction companies as well as for his own company. For the most part, his art makes you look at the humorous side of life, rarely venturing into that scary area known as reality.

Rich is a founding member of CCA.

SKETCHING IN CLAY. Next to stone (and some cheeses), wood is one of the more difficult media for sculpture.

With this in mind, a carver should use technologies available to him or her to end up with a decent piece of work. My pencil sketching abilities are limited, so I tend to sketch three dimensionally in clay. I'll start by pushing around very small pieces of clay to get the feel for the action I want in the carving. After I've decided on the position and the proportions of the piece I will begin an actual size sculpture.

FIRST THE CLAY. Dave Dunham sent me his completed piano player in order for me to match his scale. I cut a piece of wood the size of the piano and used that as a base for my sculpture. I do most of my human figures nude to begin with and then slowly bring myself to clothing when the anatomy is where I want it.

I've always felt that concept is the most important part of my work. To get from the concept to the finished piece with the least amount of variance, you have to work out the anatomy, action, character and so forth in clay first, that's how it is for us non-geniuses anyway. Without going into the fine details, I can then use my sculpture for a side-view pattern to begin my woodcarving. The ultimate goal would be to duplicarve it at this point, but I don't have one of those big machines.

THEN THE WOOD. I begin by blocking out the pattern in one dimension with a band saw. Just follow the dotted lines around the pattern. Most of the carving, probably 80 percent, is done with a knife. I use gouges only for the finish detail.

I used my clay model as a reference throughout the project, which I find extremely helpful and beneficial. There will always be some difference between the two, some better, some worse. In this particular case, I liked my clay model much more than the final carving. I lost some action, and the piece ended up being slightly larger than intended. Wood is a tough medium and can sometimes fall short of what you originally had in mind, but it has rewards that can't be found in other forms of sculpture.

PAINTING AND FINISHING. I prefer to paint my carvings with light washes of acrylics. The key here is light washes (heard that before?). Water 'em down. The only exception is that I use full strength colors for eye detail. When the painting is completed, I seal the carving with Krylon Matte Finish (spray-on type), then antique it with a one to one mixture of Folkart Antiquing and water.

Full Moon Saloon

Full Moon Saloon

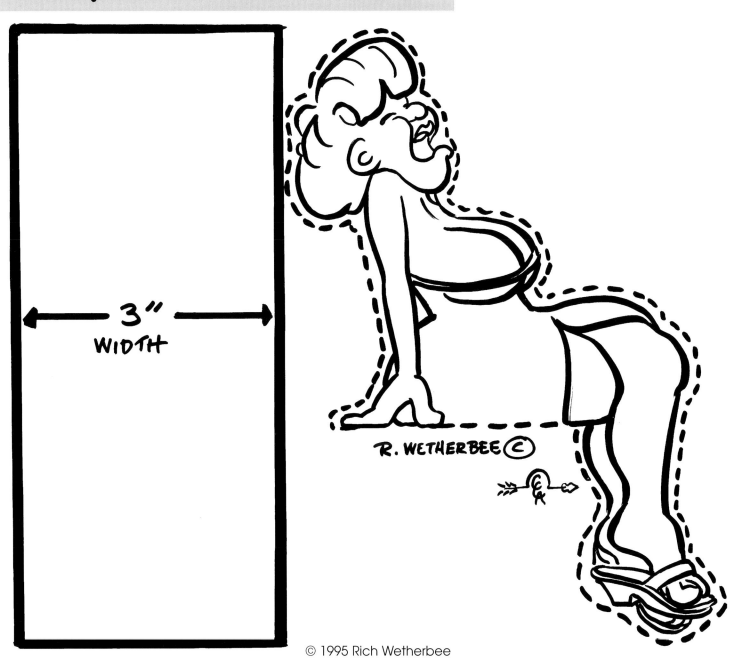

Man's Best Friend by Tom Wolfe

Tom began carving at the age of 12. Today, he has become one of America's most recognized and respected carvers. A resident of West Jefferson, North Carolina, Tom has helped thousands of people develop their skills. In addition to teaching, he has written many books—more than 20 at last count. His approach to teaching through his books is straight forward. He leads the reader, step-by-step, through the carving process. His books have been well received from the newest learner to the most seasoned veteran, because of the simple methods and obvious enjoyment Tom brings to his art. Tom sells his original work, as well as cast models and a series of cast characters he created for finer gift stores.

First, some notes on the subject of Self. The earliest I remember doing art work (not counting drawing in my older brother and sister's school books) was before I started school, around 4 or 5. I would dig clay out of the hill behind the house to make animals and then dry them in the sun on the flat rock that was used to cover the well. I think the rock was put there to keep me out. When my animals were good and dry, I would play with them until they broke and then make more.

THE FIRST WOODCARVING. I don't remember it, but one of my patterns in my book *Basic Penknife Carving* is of a piece that I carved in the 7th grade (1951). My first show was the 1953 Scholastic Art Show in Charleston, West Virginia. I won two gold keys. Even though I did attend one semester at the American Institute of Art at Chicago, I haven't had enough formal training to interfere with my art.

WOOD. The most often asked question is "What is the best wood to carve?" I could probably write a book on that one because it is the hardest one to answer. My answer is free wood. With my "slight" southern drawl, most people respond with, "Did you say tree wood?" No, I mean free wood. Seriously though, in this case the end dictates the beginning. If it is to be painted, I use basswood or another wood that accepts paint well most of the time.

TOOLS: I use a long-handled knife of my own design. The shaped blades shown in this illustration seem to do most of the work.

In addition to my knife, I used a set of palm gouges for this project. The most important tip is to keep them sharp. The only thing worse than not having the right tools is not having sharp tools. One other point. When I say sharp tools, I mean sharp enough to shave with!

PATTERNS. You will find patterns not only for this project, but also for other dogs.

CARVING. Now to the carving of the dog. Before someone asks, I never do a

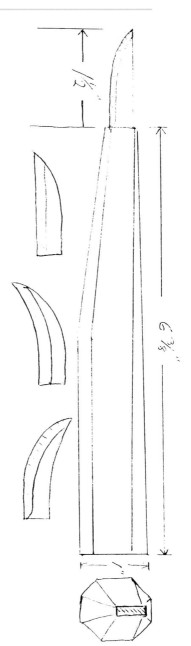

Full Moon Saloon

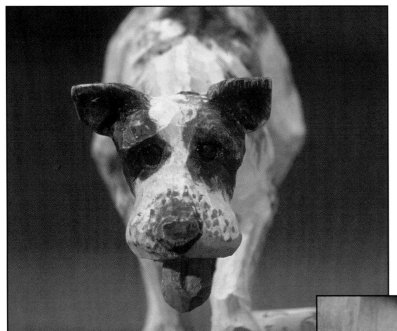

two-sided cut-out. It just doesn't work for me. I teach the way I carve, and what I want is movement. My patterns are drawn from the most difficult profile; in this case, the side profile. When making a template pattern, I make it the correct size and saw on the line. Do not overcompensate. This way the silhouette need never be cut out. From this square blank, I use the drill press with Forstner bits to drill off large unwanted masses (like unwanted legs and the such). From this square pattern, carve to an octagon. From here on out the old joke, "Cut off everything that doesn't look like a dog," applies.

FINISHING. Finally, a bit on painting. I like oil paint. I mix it in an eight ounce juice bottle: about a one-inch worm of paint to about $1/4$ of the bottle of turpentine. Remember to mix it well. This mixture will keep a long time, just shake it well before using it. What this system amounts to is painting with a stain, and it gives a light touch of color that needs no antiquing.

"Cut off everything that doesn't look like a dog," an old addage that many carvers use for carving a variety of topics, fits Tom Wolfe's caricature Man's Best Friend. *The dog tries in vain to raise Harold Enlow's cowboy,* Flat On His Back.

104

Man's Best Friend by Tom Wolfe

105

Three Painting Techniques

Bob Travis carved, painted and antiqued this caricature to demonstrate the use of acrylic washes. Step-by-step photos of his techniques appear on pages 107–108.

Painting adds the final touch to a caricature carving and, if done properly, can literally bring the carving to life. Most caricature carvers prefer light washes of either acrylic or oil colors. Marv Kaisersatt is an exception to the rule as he prefers to leave his carvings unpainted. His contribution to the Full Moon Saloon, *The Seated Cowboy* (See pages 38-41.), was painted in order to fit in with the rest of the carvings.

Whether one uses acrylic or oil paints the results are similar, but the techniques can vary considerably. The main difference in the two systems is the difference in drying times for acrylics and oils. Acrylic washes tend to dry fairly quickly and once they dry on wood they are there to stay. Blending of colors on wood is possible, but this is most effective when colors are blended wet-on-wet (when the under color is still wet). Light washes can be darkened by adding additional coats. Oils, on the other hand, dry slowly and can be blended on wood fairly effectively.

The examples cited in this chapter are representative of the techniques used by the carvers featured in this book. Bob's card player with a hand over his face, his drunk cowboy on the balcony, and the girl in the card game were painted with acrylic washes. Desiree's horse sitting at the bar was painted with acrylics using the wet-on-wet technique. Lastly, Pete LeClair's two cowboys standing at the bar were painted with oil washes. This discussion is not intended to be an all-inclusive treatise on painting. Rather we suggest that you experiment with both acrylics and oils and develop a system that best meets your needs. Regardless of the method that you decide upon, the key is to apply dilute washes. Many excellent carvings have been ruined by applying too much paint.

ACRYLIC WASHES. Acrylic washes can be applied directly to bare wood without sealing. Before painting, wash the entire carving with a tooth brush wetted with a sudsy mix of 2-3 drops of liquid dish detergent in a glass of warm water. This will remove oil and dirt that will show through light paint washes. Rinse with warm water and blot dry immediately with paper towels. The carving can be painted before it dries, but it is best to let it set overnight before painting.

Flesh tones can be prepared by mixing white with a small amount of red, a smaller amount of yellow, and a trace of blue, but this can be a tedious process and it is often difficult to reproduce the end product. Commercially available

1. All the flesh-colored areas on the caricature have been painted.

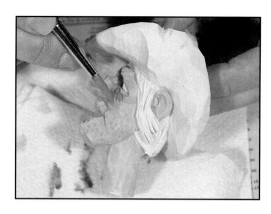

2. Bob adds a blush color to the cheeks by blending cadmium red medium into the flesh color while it is still wet.

3. A small dot of white is added to each blue eye to show a reflection spot in the eye.

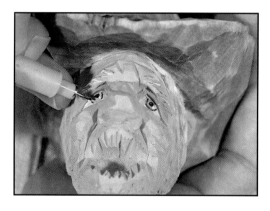

4. To create the black line around the iris, Bob uses a pen filled with permanent ink.

5. Bob adds gray streaks to the hair with a small brush.

6. A light wash of ultramarine blue is used to color the pants. The cowboy's shirt has already been painted with the same color.

PHOTOS BY SHIRLEY COFFELT, SACRAMENTO, CA

107

Full Moon Saloon

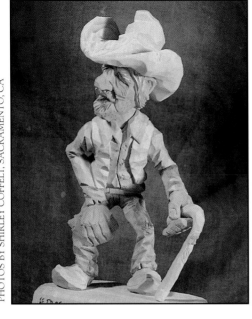

108

7. This photo shows the caricature with the face, hair, pants and shirt painted.

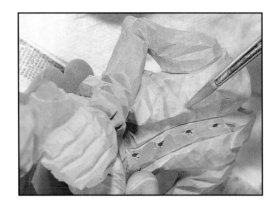

8. Using a light wash of raw sienna, Bob paints the vest next.

9. He paints the base of the carving with a light wash of burnt umber.

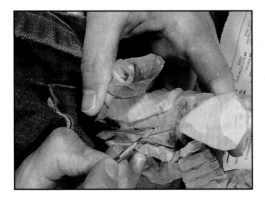

10. To paint the buttons on the cowboy's shirt, Bob uses ultramarine blue straight from the tube.

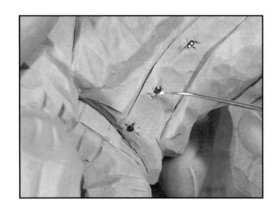

11. Again using the paint straight from the tube, Bob applies small dots of white for the button thread.

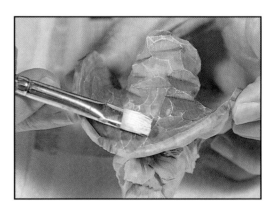

12. With a stiff bristled brush, Bob dry brushes the hat with Titanium white. The pants and shirt have also been dry brushed in the same manner. When the paint is dry, Bob will antique the carving.

flesh tones (CeramCoat by Delta) eliminate these problems. Apply the flesh tone a little thicker than the other colors so that the antiquing (described below) doesn't darken the face and hands. Be certain that all of the flesh is covered or the antiquing will leave dark spots where the wood is unpainted. This is usually not a problem on clothing, but when it happens on the nose, earlobe or other critical places it can be distracting. Bob uses two flesh shades, medium and dark. Medium is good for a girl's face, but a little light for a crusty old range-worn cowboy. For his face, mix about 1/3 dark with medium flesh to give a ruddy, sunburned look. Add about three parts water to one part paint. Paint the entire face, including the eyebrows, eyes and teeth, but not the hair. If you paint hair with the flesh tone it will not take another color unless that color is put on very thick. Be sure to paint all flesh at this stage. Don't forget toes sticking out of shoes, and flesh that is exposed through holes and tears in the clothing. Add a little rosy blush to the cheek, lips and chin by first rewetting a small area with a dilute mix of the flesh tone then rapidly blending in a tiny dab of Crimson Red Medium. It is easy to get too much red, so practice the technique on a scrap of wood to avoid ruining the carving. Use the same technique with Ultramarine Blue to add shadow above the eyes on female faces. Experiment with other blush and eye shadow colors. Some carvers will blend dark flesh on medium flesh, using the wet-on-wet technique (described below), to obtain a tanned look on the high spots of the face and hands.

Paint the eyeballs and teeth with white directly from a tube. Liquitex colors work well, but

other brands are also suitable. CeramCoat, and other bottled colors are not thick enough to cover the flesh tone. Paint the iris of the eye with a blended color, also directly from the tube. Ultramarine Blue, Hooker's Green, or Burnt Umber lightened with white are good eye colors. Be sure to add plenty of white. When an eye is opened you usually see only the bottom two thirds or so of the iris, unless the expression is one of surprise with the eyes wide opened. Add a dot of black for the pupil and a tiny speck of white for the light reflection. Finish the eye by drawing a black line around the iris with a permanent drawing pen. Water soluble ink will run when the antiquing is applied. Use the same pen to add eye-

Peter Ribbit, a caricature carving of a frog wearing a rabbit mask, was carved by Desiree Hajny. Desiree demonstrates her wet-on-wet painting techniques on pages 110–111.

109

1. Desiree applies a light wash of pink acrylic paint over the frog's rabbit mask. This wash will serve as an undercoat for the other colors.

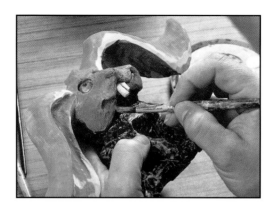

2. While the paint is still wet, Desiree applies additional shades of pink to show highlights and shadows. A darker shade is applied under the chin and blended into the wet paint underneath.

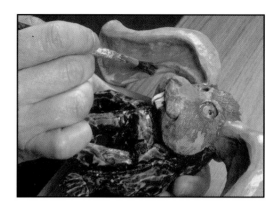

3. Dark shades are blended in on the inside of the ear. Lighter shades have been applied to areas where light will create a highlight.

4. The various acrylics applied with the wet-on-wet technique are allowed to dry.

5. Desiree uses a stiff bristled brush to dry brush white highlights onto the mask.

6. To ready her brush for dry brushing, Desiree dips her brush into the paint, scrubs it on the paint palette to remove excess paint from the brush, and then draws the brush across the texture of the wood.

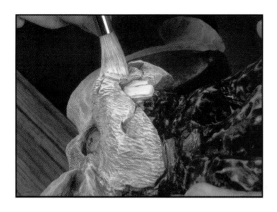

7. Pulling the brush across the texture of the wood keeps the color on the high spots only.

8. The pink paint can be seen through the white because the white paint rests on the raised texture and does not sink into the low spots where the pink paint still shows.

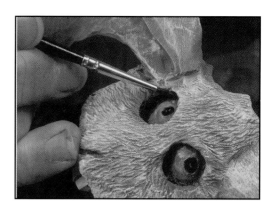

9. With a small pointed brush, or a spotter, Desiree paints the ring on the inside of the mask.

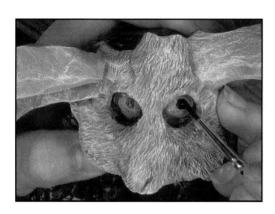

10. Again using the spotter brush, Desiree paints the pupil. Because the frog is wearing a mask, his eyes, and not the brown eyes of a rabbit, show through the mask.

11. The spotter brush is also used to apply a highlight to the eye.

12. Final details, such as freckles and eye brows, are added after the rest of the painting is finished.

Pete LeClair carved and painted this cowboy to demonstrate his use of oil paints. Step-by-step photos of his techniques are shown on pages 113–114.

brows and lashes to a female face. The card playing girl was purposely given a "hard" look by accentuating the eyebrows and adding bright red lipstick.

Additional colors are made up by diluting a small amount (about the size of a pea) of acrylic paint from a tube in about 1/8 cup of water. Bottled colors also work, but they should not be diluted as much. Test each color on a block of wood before using to make certain it is the desired shade. Brighter colors are desirable on female carvings so the "light" washes used on the girl contained a little more paint, perhaps half again as much per unit water as used on the cowboys. The key is to not mix the paint too thick or the antiquing will not be effective. A good rule of thumb is to dilute the color until you think it is ready, then dilute it some more. Black is especially tricky as a little dab goes a long ways. If the color is too light, it can be darkened by adding additional coats, but if you get it on too dark it cannot be lightened. Begin with the inside clothing and work outward.

Hair can be painted with the same tech-niques used on clothing. You can enhance the hair a bit on "older" cowboys by streaking it with lighter colors. Start by making a relatively thick mixture of the hair color then blend in a little white. Add a few streaks to the hair from the top down with a stiff fine tip brush. Blend in a little more white and repeat the process using care not to cover all of the first streaking coat. This will produce an overlay effect that gives the look of graying hair. Paint eyebrows by lightly lining on thick mixtures of the base hair color followed by the same colors that are used for streaking.

Use unthinned paint directly from the tube for buttons, button thread, polka dots, etc. Dry-brushed colors are also applied directly from the tube. Use a stiff, flat tip brush for dry-brushing. Dab on a small amount of white then vigorously brush off excess paint on a paper towel. Next, lightly brush across areas to be dry-brushed. This technique works especially well on hair, blue jeans, and dark colored hats and boots. Again, experiment first because it is easy to ruin a carving by applying too much paint.

ACRYLICS APPLIED WET-ON-WET. Desiree also uses acrylic colors but her technique is more of a wet-on-wet process than the system described above. Her approach is similar to the watercolor wet-on-wet system except that the first applica-tion (the undercoat) is of paint rather than water.

The colors are applied in a watery, or milky, consistency that is considerably thicker than those used in the acrylic technique described above. The different colors are applied to the wood surface and allowed to touch and blend together. Place small dabs of desired colors on a

1. Pete's cowboy is fully carved and ready for oil paints. He starts with the eyes, belt buckle, T-shirt and button.

2. Next, Pete applies a base coat to the entire carving.

3. In this photo, the carving has been completely covered with the base coat.

4. Once the base coat has dried, Pete applies flesh tone to the cowboy's face and hands.

5. For the cheeks, Pete uses a small amount of Grumbacher red placed on the cheek area, then blended with pure linseed oil. The lips are Grumbacher red with a small amount of burnt sienna mixed in. Again, the color is blended on the carving with linseed oil.

6. Pete paints the cowboy's hair with burnt sienna mixed with a small amount of brown.

CARICATURE CARVERS of AMERICA

7. Pete paints the cowboy's shirt with Grumbacher red. The hat has been painted with black.

8. Using Cobalt blue, Pete paints the cowboy's pants. The belt was painted with black.

9. Last, Pete paints the cowboy's boots. He uses a mixture of Alizarin crimson and green to make brown.

114

palate and, working with a wet brush, pull out small amounts of paint and blend directly on the carving. Since the acrylics dry quickly the colors must be applied quickly. Take it section by section (example: head area, neck, shoulders, front legs, body, hips, tail, and back legs). The paint is absorbed into the wood like a stain. Allow to dry.

Dry-brushing on a highlight color will add a nice finishing touch by enhancing the texture that you have created. Using a stiff-bristled brush, scrub the color into the brush and pull it gently in the opposite direction of the texture.

Finally, use a spotter brush to add details like eyes, nose, hooves, etc.

ARTIST'S OIL WASHES. Oil washes can be applied to wood carvings much the same way that acrylic washes are used. Pete begins by coating the entire carving with a prestain prepared by dissolving a small amount of Raw Sienna in 8 oz. linseed oil. Dissolve the paint in the oil by vigorously shaking the mixture for several seconds. Test on a scrap of basswood. The stain should turn the wood a pale yellow, like the color of Eastern Pine. The desired end result is a transparent finish that allows the wood grain to remain visible.

All other stains are prepared by mixing a small amount of paint in linseed oil. Pete usually keeps 20 to 30 premixed colors on hand. Place 3/4 oz. or so, of linseed oil in a 1 1/2 ounce plastic bottle, add a small amount of oil color, cover and shake well. Test on a piece of basswood that has had the base coat applied. If the color is too light, add a little more paint to the mixture; if the color is too dark, add a little more linseed oil.

Flesh tones require a little extra effort in mixing. Pete's recipe is as follows: add a small amount of Zinc White to 3/4 ounce linseed oil and shake well. Next add a very small amount of Alizarin Crimson to the mixture and shake again. Finally, add a small amount of Burnt Sienna and shake. Test this mixture on a base-coated piece of basswood. Continue to add Burnt Sienna, a little at a time, until the desired skin tone is achieved.

Begin by painting the eyes and teeth, as well as buttons, belt buckles, etc., with acrylics. Oil colors will work, but they must be put on fairly thick and will bleed together as you paint adjacent areas. Acrylics dry quickly and you can begin adding other colors soon after finishing the eyes. The rest of the carving is stained with the linseed oil washes much the same way as acrylic washes are applied.

As an alternative method you might try using odorless turpanoid in place of the linseed oil. Coat the entire carving with turpanoid then apply the stain coats as above. This also works well when the paint is applied directly from a palate using a brush wetted with turpanoid. One advantage to this latter method is that the intensity of colors can be easily changed even after they are on the wood. If the color is too light, blend in a little more paint. If the color is too dark it can be lightened by brushing more turpanoid into the wood.

ANTIQUING MIXTURES. There are probably as many antiquing recipes as there are caricature carvers. It seems as though everyone has a favorite formula. For several years Bob used a mixture of eight parts natural and two parts medium walnut Watco oil. Unfortunately, oil based Watco oil is no longer being made. Apparently it will be replaced with an acrylic formulation and we are not certain how well that will work. An alternative is to use boiled linseed oil that has had the color enhanced with a small amount of artist's oil paint.

The following recipe is recommended by Steve Prescott: squeeze about one inch of artist's oil (burnt umber of raw umber) from a tube into one quart of boiled linseed oil and mix thoroughly. Steve recommends using an old blender as the paint is difficult to mix into the oil. A word of warning though, don't use a good blender or you will be in the market for a new one. One advantage to Watco Oil is that it dries much faster than the linseed oil mixture. To alleviate this problem, Steve recommends adding about a cup of mineral spirits to the recipe to hasten drying. Dip the entire carving in the antiquing mix, or apply amply with a brush or sponge, and blot dry with paper towels. The overall effect will be a softening and darkening of the bright, sometimes chalky appearing colors. This mixture will work on both acrylic and oil stained carvings.

Caution: Use care in disposing of the used towels as they may ignite spontaneously. For maximum safety it is best to submerge all waste material in water and leave wet until removed from the premises. Also make sure to work in an area with adequate ventilation to prevent breathing of harmful fumes.

Fox Chapel Publishing

How-To and Reference Books from the Experts

Woodworking Titles

Easy to Make Wooden Inlay Projects: Intarsia
New second edition. Full color project gallery. Includes 12 ready to use patterns.
Intarsia is a method of making picture mosaics in wood, using a combination of wood grains and colors. The techniques and step-by-step instructions in this book will have you completing your own beautiful pieces in short order. Written by acknowledged expert Judy Gale Roberts, who has her own studio and publishes the Intarsia Times newsletter, produces videos, gives seminars and writes articles on the Intarsia method. Each project is featured in full color and this well written, heavily illustrated features over 100 photographs and includes index and directory of suppliers. New second edition features 30 projects in color.

ISBN# 56523-023-X   200 pages, soft cover, 8.5 x 11 inches $19.95

Making Collector Plates on Your Scroll Saw
by Judy Gale Roberts
Hot new title from Judy Gale Roberts (best-selling author of Easy to Make Inlay Wood Projects-INTARSIA). Make personalized commemorative plates for birthdays, weddings anniversaries and other special events.. Easy to follow techniques to make and finish 10 ready to use patterns. Full color on every page. 40+ color photos soft cover, full color, 64 pages

ISBN # 1-56523-050-7
$12.95 retail

More great scroll saw books by Judy Gale Roberts!
Fine Line Designs Scroll Saw Fretwork Patterns

Especially designed for the scroll saw enthusiast who wishes to excel, the 'fine line design' method helps you to control drift error found with thick line patterns. Each book features great designs, expert tips, and patterns on oversized (up to 11" x 17" !) sheets in a special "lay flat" spiral binding. Choose the original Design Book 1 with animal and fun designs, or Design Book Two featuring "Western- Southwestern" designs.

Scroll Saw Fretwork Pattern, Design Book One "The Original"
$14.95
Scroll Saw Fretwork Patterns, Design Book Two "Western-Southwestern" $16.95

Scroll Saw Fretwork Patterns, Design Book Three
" The Great Outdoors" Patterns for a variety of wildlife, hunting and fishing scenes. $14.95

Scroll Saw Fretwork Patterns, Design Book Four
"Sports". Patterns for almost every type of sport activity - baseball, football, basketball ... and more.

$14.95
Scroll Saw Fretwork Patterns, Design Book Five
"Heartland- Farm & Country". Great country woodworking designs and scenes. $14.95

Scroll Saw Fretwork Patterns, Design Book Six
" Pets & People" Creative patterns for dog, cat and pet-lovers. $14.95

Scroll Saw Woodcrafting Magic! Complete Pattern and How-to Manual (2nd revised printing)
Includes complete patterns drawn to scale. You will be amazed at how easy it is to make these beautiful projects when you follow Joanne's helpful tips and work from these clear, precise patterns. Never-before-published patterns for original and creative toys, jewelry, and gifts. Never used a scroll saw? The tutorials in this book will get you started quickly. Experienced scroll-sawyers will delight in these all-new, unique projects, perfect for craft sales and gift-giving. Written by Joanne Lockwood, owner of Three Bears Studio in California and the president of the Sacramento Area Woodworkers; she is frequently featured in national woodwork and craft magazines.

ISBN# 1-56523-024-8   300 pages, soft cover, 8.5 x 11 inches $16.95 retail

The Mott Miniature Furniture Workshop Manual
by Barbara and Elizabeth Mott
THE book for miniature furniture hobbyists. Jam-packed with techniques and patterns. Contains ready to use detailed patterns for 144 projects- from windsor chairs to rocking horses-all to scale. Information on miniature chair caning, wood bending, assembly instructions carving techniques. Over 100 ready to use miniature prints, photos and decals included.
Soft cover, 220 pages

ISBN# 1-56523-052-3 $19.95 retail

Woodcarving Titles

Woodcarvers Workbook - Carving Animals with Mary Duke Guldan
" Best Woodcarving pattern book I've seen in my 40 years as a carver"
Ed Gallenstein, President National Woodcarvers Association
These complete step-by-step instructionas and easy to follow patterns will guide you through the process of creating beautiful handcarved masterpieces of your own. Woodcarvers Workbook is chock-full ofinteresting notes, expert tips and solid information. Twelve patterns included for moose, bear, dog, wild horses, cougar, rabbits and more. Painting and finishing section.

ISBN #1-56523-033-7   softcover 96 pages $14.95 retail

Second Woodcarvers Workbook
by Mary Duke Guldan
Long-awaited second book by acclaimed woodcarving author and National Woodcarving Association columnist. Easy to follow instructions accompany the best carving patterns available any where. Patterns include: Native Indian Chief, wild animals, farm animals, Texas Longhorn 12 + patterns in all.
Soft cover 96 pages

ISBN # 1-56523-037-X $14.95 retail

The Fantastic Book of Canes, Pipes and Walking Sticks
by Harry Ameredes
Veteran carver Ameredes has included hundreds of original designs from 35 years of his work in his exciting sketchbook for woodcarvers and cane collectors. Includes plans for using driftwood and tree roots to make fabulous one-of-a-kind carvings.
Soft cover 128 pages

ISBN # 1-56523-048-5 $12.95 retail

Woodcarving Adventure Movie Caricatures
with Jim Maxwell
Jim Maxwell turns his creative eye to carving caricatures of our favorite movie stars. Create your own striking carvings of John Wayne, Indiana Jones and others. Heavily illustrated with over 225 photos of step-by-step instructions and finished projects. Sure to appeal to both beginning and advanced carvers. 12 ready to use patterns included
Soft cover, 128 pages

ISBN # 1-56523-051-5 $12.95 retail

Making Collectible Santas and Christmas Ornametns in Wood

by Jim and margie Maxwell

These 42 easy to follow projects ill make you very popular this Christmas! Full size patterns included for a Snowman, 10 different Santas, Nutcracker ornament and more. 48 pages.

    Order #Maxwell1

    $6.95

Carving Characters with Jim Maxwell

Want to learn how to carve folk characters in wood? This book shows you how from start to finish. In step-by-step photos and instructions, Jim makes it easy. Twelve different project patterns included.

    Order #Maxwell2

    $6.95

Carving Decorative Fish by Jim Jensen

26 detailed patterns for favorite fresh and salt water fish projects accompany an excellent step-by-step technique and photo section that leaves nothing to guess work. Painting how-to section in full color.

Soft cover, 128 pages, b/w and color photos

    ISBN # 1-56523-053-1

    $14.95 retail

Mammals: An Artistic Approach by Desiree Hajny

Your chance to learn from one of the world's top notch carvers. Features a helpful step-by-step photo session as Desiree carvers an otter. Learn the carving, texturing and painting techniques that have brought worldwide recognition of her work. Patterns, anatomy studies and reference photos are inside for deer, bears, otters and more. Color section PLUS a gallery section showing some of her outstanding pieces over the years. Heavily illustrated Softcover, 180 pages.

    Available NOW   ISBN # 1-56523-036-1 $19.95 retail

Carving Wooden Critters

Includes power carving techniques by Diane Ernst

Diane Ernst's first pattern treasury. A frequent award winner for her cute puppies, rabbits and other critters, Diane's patterns feature multiple views-top, side, front and back and also include wood burning details. A step by step photo session using power carving tools is also included. Buy this book and start carving your own character-filled critters.

    Available NOW   ISBN # 1-56523-038-8 $6.95 retail

Carving Kids with Ivan Whillock

Brand new title from the author of pictorial Relief Carving, and Carving the Head in Wood. Master carver Whillock now turns his talents to carving an engaging series of children's portraits at play - playing baseball, dressing up in Mommy's clothes - ten different projects. Carving techniques are illustrated step-by-step, PLUS complete patterns are included. Full color project gallery. Over 100 illustrations.

    Available NOW   ISBN# 1-56523-045-0 $12.95 retail

Cowtown Carving-by Steve Prescott

Texas Whittling Champion Steve Prescott's collection of 15 original caricature projects features full size plans and excellent instructions for carving and finishing.

Soft cover, 96 pages

    $14.95

    ISBN # 1-56523-049-3   Available NOW

Woodcarving Books by George Lehman

Learn new techniques as you carve these projects designed by professional artists and carver George Lehman. These best-selling books by a master carver are invaluable reference books, PLUS each book contains over 20 ready-to-use patterns.

Book One - Carving Realistic Game and Songbirds - Patterns and instructions

Enthusiastically received by carvers across the US and Canada. George pays particular attention to the needs of beginning carvers in this volume. 20 patterns, over 70 photos, sketches and reference drawing.

    ISBN# 1-56523-004-3   96 pages, spiral bound, 14 x 11 inches, includes index, resources $19.95

Book Two - Realism in Wood - 22 projects, detailed patterns and instructions

This volume features a selection of patterns for shorebirds and birds of prey in addition to all-new duck and songbird patterns. Special sections on adding detail, burning.

    ISBN# 1-56523-005-1,   112 pages, spiral bound, 14 x 11 inches, includes index, resources $19.95

Book Three - Nature in Wood - patterns for carving 21 smaller birds and 8 wild animals

Focuses on songbirds and small game birds . Numerous tips and techniques throughout including instruction on necessary skills for creating downy feather details and realistic wings. Wonderful section on wild animal carvings with measured patterns.

    ISBN #1-56523-006-X   128 pages, soft bound, 11 x 8.5 inches, includes index, resources $16.95

Book Four - Carving Wildlife in Wood- 20 Exciting Projects

Here is George's newest book for decorative woodcarvers with never-before-published patterns. Tremendously detailed, these patterns appeal to carvers at all skill levels. Patterns for birds of prey, ducks, wild turkey, shorebirds and more! Great addition to any carvers library - will be used again and again.

    ISBN #1-56523-007-8   96 pages, spiral-bound, 14 x 11 $19.95

Encyclopedia of Bird Reference Drawings

by David Mohrhardt

This helpful reference features detailed sketches and wing studies for more than 215 different birds. Includes lots of hard-to-find information. Mohrhardt is an award-winning artist. This book contains much material that he gathered for use in his own work. We recommend this book as an excellent general reference for all carvers, bird lovers and artists. Recommended by Bob Guge, World Champion Carver.

    ISBN #1-56523-009-4   96 pages $14.95

Fox Chapel Publishing Co Inc.

To order, please send check or money order for price listed plus $2.50 per book postage.

Send to:

Fox Chapel Book Orders

Box 7948B

Lancaster, PA 17604

1(800) 457-9112

Fax (717) 560-4702

Please try your favorite book supplier first!

Books from the Experts!
Fox Chapel Publishing

*Carving the Full Moon Saloon with the Caricature Carvers of America. Patterns ideas and techniques from some of the best carvers alive- Harold Enlow, Tom Wolfe, Desiree Hajny, Steve Prescott, Pete LeClair, Bob Travis and 15 more. Over 100 color photos show close up details, painting tips and more. THE book for caricature carvers. Available June '95 **$19.95**

Frank Russell Titles

*Carving Weathered Wood and Natural Materials with Frank Russell. Full color guide to carving with natural and found materials. Includes 12 projects for weathered wood, antlers, bone, eggs and more. Available July '95 **$14.95**

*Basic Power Carving by Frank Russell. The complete guide to tools and techniques for carving with flexible shaft machines and power chisels. Includes 10 projects for birds, animals, signs and more. Full color. Available September '95 **$14.95**

*Relief Carving with Power by Frank Russell (Includes Gun Stock Checkering). Full color guide to carving beautiful relief pieces. 12 + projects, finishing tips. Nice section on gunstocks. Available September '95 **$14.95**

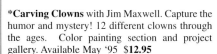

*Carving Clowns with Jim Maxwell. Capture the humor and mystery! 12 different clowns through the ages. Color painting section and project gallery. Available May '95 **$12.95**

*Bark Carving by Joyce Buchanan Full color step-by-step guide includes finishing details and 12 + patterns. Available August '95 **$12.95**

*Carving Fish- Miniature Salt water and Freshwater by Jim Jensen. These detailed patterns, woodburning tips, color painting section and step-by-step photos show you how to carve 26 different miniature fish for sale or display. Available July '95 **$14.95**

*Sculpturing Totem Poles by Walt Way This classic guide to understanding and carving totem poles is now back in print. Highly recommended. Available April '95 **$6.95**

*Small INTARSIA Projects- by Judy Gale Roberts. Full color technique and pattern manual featuring 12 + new patterns for jewelry, small boxes and more! Available in September ' 95 **$14.95**

*Christian Designs for the Scroll Saw Inside are 100 + patterns for jewelry, ornaments, plaques, crosses and more. These precise drawings could be used for relief carving and pierced carvings as well. 30 projects in color. available August '95 **$12.95**

*Mott Miniature Furniture Workshop Manual. Ready to use patterns for 144 projects 220 pages. Available July '95 **$19.95**

Books Available Now
Caricature & Animal Carving

Animal Books by Chip Chats columnist Mary Duke Guldan.
Woodcarvers Workbook-Carving Animals with Mary Duke Guldan. Step-by-Step instructions and the best patterns you've ever seen! 9 patterns- including Wolves, Whitetails, Wild Horses, Moose, Rabbit, Dogs. **$14.95**

Woodcarver's Workbooks #2- More Great Projects No repeats from book #1 above- patterns including Buffalo, Bears, Elk, Native Chief, Horses, Mules, Oxen . . . and more **$14.95**

Mammals: An Artistic Approach by desiree Hajny. Step by step photographs and color painting section teach you Desiree's secrets to her world class carving. Patterns included for otter, bear, deer **$19.95**

Fantastic Book of Canes, Pipes and Walking Sticks by Harry Ameredes. 100's of detailed designs. Including weathered wood tree-root designs and pipes. **$12.95**

Making Collectible Santas and Christmas Ornaments. 42 easy to follow projects. Hand-carved ornaments are popular! **$6.95**

Carving Characters with Jim Maxwell. Twelve favorite projects from the Ozark Mountains **$6.95**

Carving Wooden Critters by Diane Ernst 16 projects and step-by-step section. Rabbits, puppies, otters &more in her unique caricature style. Great designs! **$6.95**

Carving Kids- Ivan Whillock Step-by-Step techniques and patterns for 12 carved children projects. **$12.95**

Woodcarving Adven-ture Movie Caricatures with Jim Maxwell. His best book yet! 150 + step by step photos. 20 + patterns. **$12.95**

Woodworking

Easy to Make Inlay Wood Projects- INTARSIA THE book on this type of relief woodworking for scroll and band saw users. 15 free patterns included, 30 projects in color. **$19.95**

Scroll Saw Woodcrafting Magic by Joanne Lockwood. 300 page project and instruction book. 30 pages of lettering and alphabets. Color painting instructions **$14.95**

Bird Carving Titles

Bird Carving Encyclopedia of Bird Reference Drawings- by Mohrhardt. Detailed sketches and info on 215 different birds. Recommended by Barth Guge. **$14.95**

George Lehman Carving books Detailed life-size patterns. For books- buy individually or save on set! 4 Book George Lehman Set (see titles below). **$69.95**

Book #1- Carving 20 Realistic Game and Songbirds. Includes loon, chickadee, owl, mallard. . . **$19.95**

Book #2- Realism in Wood- 22 patterns Special buying info, includes bald eagle, pheasants, teals. . . **$19.95**

Book #3- Nature in Wood 21 small birds and 8 animal patterns. Songbird and other small birds. Many tips and techniques. **$16.95**

Book #4- Carving Wildlife in Wood Includes shorebirds, wild turkey, geese, heron, ospray **$19.95**

How to Order: Please send price plus $2.00 per book postage (Maximum $5.00 shipping).

FOX BOOKS
Fox Chapel Publishing Co. Inc.

Fox Chapel Publishing
Box 7948
Lancaster, PA 17604-7948
FAX (717) 560-4702
Toll Free Order Desk- 1(800) 457 0112

You are invited to Join the

National Wood Carvers Association

"Some carve their careers: others just chisel"

since 1953

If you have any interest in woodcarving: if you carve wood, create wood sculpture or even just whittle in your spare time, you will enjoy your membership in the National Wood Carvers Association. The non-profit NWCA is the world's largest carving club with over 33,000 members. There are NWCA members in more than 56 countries around the globe.

The Association's goals are to:

- promote wood carving
- foster fellowship among member enthusiasts
- encourage exhibitions and area get togethers
- list sources of equipment and information for the wood carving artist
- provide a forum for carving artists

The NWCA serves as a valuable network of tips, hints and helpful information for the wood carver. Membership is only $11.00 per year.

Members receive the magazine "Chip Chats" six times a year, free with their membership. "Chip Chats" contains articles, news events, demonstrations of technique, patterns and a full color section showcasing examples of fine craftsmanship. Through this magazine you will be kept up to date on shows and workshops to attend, new products, special offers to NWCA members and other members' activities in your area and around the world.

National Wood Carvers Association

7424 Miami Ave.
Cincinnati, OH 45243

Name: _____

Address: _____

_____

Dues $11.00 per year in USA, $14.00 per year foreign (payable in US Funds)